YOU DON'T NEED A MAN!

Why You Don't Need to Settle and How To Find A High-Quality Man

Written By: Lana Otoya

©2019

YOU DON'T NEED A MAN!

Copyright © 2019 by Lana Otoya

All rights reserved. This book or any portion thereof may not be reproduced or used in any manner whatsoever without the express written permission of the publisher except for the use of brief quotations in a book review.

The content contained within this book may not be reproduced, duplicated or transmitted without direct written permission from the author or the publisher.

Under no circumstances will any blame or legal responsibility be held against the publisher, or author, for any damages, reparation, or monetary loss due to the information contained within this book. Either directly or indirectly.

Printed in the United States of America

First Printing, 2019

Author contact:

Lana Otoya

Millennialships.com

Legal Notice:

This book is copyright protected. This book is only for personal use. You cannot amend, distribute, sell, use, quote or paraphrase any part, or the content within this book, without the consent of the author or publisher.

Disclaimer Notice:

Please note the information contained within this document is for educational and entertainment purposes only. All effort has been executed to present accurate, up to date, and reliable, complete information. No warranties of any kind are declared or implied. Readers acknowledge that the author is not engaging in the rendering of legal, financial, medical or professional advice. The content within this book has been derived from various sources. Please consult a licensed professional before attempting any techniques outlined in this book. By reading this document, the reader agrees that under no circumstances is the author responsible for any losses, direct or indirect, which are incurred as a result of the use of information contained within this document, including, but not limited to, — errors, omissions, or inaccuracies.

DEDICATION

This book is dedicated to the three people who taught me everything I know about romantic love. My first boyfriend - who taught me that you can have chemistry with someone who is really mean. My second boyfriend -who taught me that no matter how hard you try; you can't change someone. And my current boyfriend- who taught me that the tall, dark, handsome and loving man we all dream about actually exists.

Your Free Gift

Don't get stuck with a loser again!

Download my FREE *Dating Red Flags Checklist* so you know how to look for a high-quality man.

Visit: millennialships.com/red-flags

Table Of Contents

YOU DON'T NEED A MAN! i
Why You Don't Need to Settle and How To Find A High-Quality Man i

DEDICATION vi

Your Free Gift viii

Table Of Contents ix

INTRODUCTION 11
A Letter From The Author 11

CHAPTER ONE 16
The Fisherwoman and The Coal Miner 16

CHAPTER TWO 21
You Don't Need Fish, Steak Is Good Too 21

CHAPTER THREE 42
Being Single: The Good, The Bad and Too Much Netflix 42

CHAPTER FOUR 59
The Dating Lens and The Mindset of Success 59

CHAPTER FIVE 81
The Emotions of Dating 81

CHAPTER SIX 109

CHAPTER SEVEN	**148**
How To Find The One Who Is Worth Your Time	*148*
CHAPTER EIGHT	**194**
Needs and Wants	*194*
ABOUT THE AUTHOR	**197**
Your Free Gift	**198**
Works Cited	**199**

INTRODUCTION

A Letter From The Author

THE FACT THAT YOU OPENED THIS BOOK IS A dream come true. I've always been passionate about human behavior and relaying the information I learned to others. I studied human behavior for fun, in school and learned about romantic relationships in order to try and save a very unhealthy one that was completely unsalvageable.

Out of desperation, passion and the need to know more about human connection, I quit my corporate job to work as a matchmaker for half the paycheck. Working as a matchmaker was the best job I ever had - before I became a dating coach. It was while matchmaking that I discovered something I never truly realized. Despite having been a single woman on Tinder for many years, matchmaking taught me that people make a lot of mistakes when they're dating. My clients taught me everything I know about how different people approach dating. The things they do right, and the many (many) things they do wrong.

As a matchmaker, I loved hearing my clients' stories day after day as I helped them through their dating woes. This didn't feel like work to me, I knew I had found my calling. My passion for helping people find the love of their lives was cemented in and I started working as a dating coach. After coaching clients and hearing story after story about how miserable the dating scene can be, I decided that I could reach many more people by writing a book.

Years of research, coaching experience, and personal experience have gone into creating this book. I consider it to be the bible of all dating books. It truly covers absolutely everything you need to know in order to find someone amazing. Things like the mindset of dating, the emotions of dating, the dating game, how to text and how to find a man that is husband material. This book is my labor of love and I think you're really going to enjoy it. Before we get into the nitty-gritty though, I must clarify a couple things *right now*.

First, is that I wrote this book with Millennials in mind so there are a lot of references to Millennials and Millennial lifestyles. If you are not a Millennial, 99.9% (that's a made-up statistic) will still be relevant to you. So don't get too fussed about my references to Millennials if you are not in that generation. There's still plenty of information for you to take away.

The second is that, although I am a blogger and have written books, this book is not meant to be pretty. Any of my coaching clients will tell you, I am a blunt person and straight to the point. That's just my style. I don't like beating around the bush and I don't like fluff. This book is blunt and abrupt. You will learn something and then continue to learn something new in the following paragraph. There are not a lot of summaries or repetition. I tried my best to keep this concise and easy to read but that means you're going to get hit with a lot of information quickly.

Along with my blunt and abrupt style, I don't have time to waste on "life hack" style dating advice. This is the kind of advice you hear that goes like this: "find out exactly what to say to a man to make him swoon" or "this secret trick will make him irresistibly attached to you." Those kinds of secrets and tricks are total BS. They are not the way humans work. Those manipulative hacks are not the way humans build true connections with each other.

I prefer the scientific approach. The deep and intricate nuances of how bonds are created from one person to the next and how emotions and mindset play a role in creating chemistry and romance. Although it's a bit more of a learning curve than a "secret text" this stuff is much more fun - do you know why?

Because it actually works.

If you're ready to dive into the dating bible that I have created from scratch, I can assure you it will leave you feeling encouraged, empowered and perfectly equipped to finally find a man that is worth your time.

I know you don't have time and I'm not here to waste it. Let's get right into it my friend, this is going to be fun!

CHAPTER ONE

The Fisherwoman and The Coal Miner

"THERE ARE PLENTY OF FISH IN THE SEA." AT least that's what one of America's most popular dating sites, Plenty of Fish, wants you to believe. Although the old saying and the dating site's catchphrase may be true, most fish can be skinned, seasoned and put on a fiery grill to be enjoyed at the dinner table. A man who tears out your heart, cheats on you and breaks up with you via text message can't (legally) meet the same fate.

Before I show you how to find a tall, dark and handsome fish, it's best if we start with you, the fisherwoman. You see, dating is a *set of skills* that involves both natural temperaments and learned ability. Notice how I said it is a set of skills rather than "a" skill. This is something you shouldn't forget. Just like being the CEO of a company involves being a leader, organized and assertive; effective and healthy dating requires mental health awareness, social skills, persistence and the ability to let go. Don't worry about these skills yet, we will get to them extensively as we get through this book. For now, I want you to imagine someone.

No, not a man. I want you to imagine a woman. A strong woman who is very successful. We can call her Samantha. Samantha makes good money. She works hard, she's ambitious and she's proud of herself. She also loves the city. She likes putting on makeup, getting all dressed up and heading to a fancy restaurant for some expensive wine and a flavorful meal. Now I want you to picture a coal mine.

Yes, a coal mine. If you need help with the imagery, let me be your guide. Coal mines are long underground tunnels. They are dark, claustrophobic and *extremely* dangerous. Now I want you to imagine Samantha in this coal mine. She's never been in one before so it's totally new territory. Although a little intimidated, Samantha knows how to hold her own. The clacking, ear-shattering sound of heavy machinery doesn't faze her. Confidently, she heads down the tunnel, her white heels getting stained with dirt. She's in search of an exit. While she makes her way down, she sees a coal miner working up ahead. Seeing this coal miner as her way out, she asks him for some help.

"Hey, do you know where the exit of this mine is?" she asks.

The coal miner takes one look at Samantha and with her best interest at heart, he says to her, "you know, before you find the exit, you should probably put on the proper safety gear."

Samantha isn't too pleased with his response.

"It's alright," she tells him, "I'm just going to walk straight out; I won't be stopping along the way."

You can probably guess that Samantha has made an error here. She is so confident and sure of herself in her regular life, she isn't able to let go and accept that someone else might be the expert in this situation. She insists she knows the right answer despite being a fish out of water.

The lesson here is: don't be Samantha.

As a dating coach, I can't count the number of times someone has tried to tell me I'm wrong or I don't know this or that when it comes to dating just because they are older than me, make more money than I do or have had more bad relationships than I have. That's not easy for me to say because I know you've had your fair share of relationships. I know you've been in the dating game for a long time. I know you've been around the block and seen how it is.

If your old methods landed you a strong and healthy relationship, I would love to hear how you did it. But if your way of doing things hasn't quite worked out yet, I encourage you to take off the "I know it all" cap and put on the "learning" cap. Doing this is going to make you an expert fisherwoman. It's okay to let go and try to keep an open mind about this stuff. Instead of me catching you a fish, I can teach you how to fish...Okay, I'm done with the fish references now. I promise.

CHAPTER TWO

You Don't Need Fish, Steak Is Good Too

> *they don't want needy!*

THE TRUTH IS YOU DON'T NEED A MAN IN THE modern world. If you don't want to be an expert fisherwoman, you don't have to be. You can live a completely full and happy life on your own. Back in the old days, women *had* to get married. It was the only way they could survive. They couldn't do anything without a man, they couldn't even take out a credit card in their own name. These days, the idea of getting married isn't a necessity, it's purely a want. It's optional. If you view marriage like this, it puts you in a great place to settle down with a good long-term partner rather than settling down just for the sake of getting married. In other words, being a strong independent woman who doesn't need a man, puts you in a position to have a very successful marriage or long-term relationship.

YOU'RE NOT WEIRD FOR BEING SINGLE

The reality is, if you are starting to think about settling down after you established your career, you are not alone. Most Millennials, both men and women are doing that. An article from the New York Times talked about research that was done on Millennial views on marriage and relationships. It said:

"Sociologists, psychologists and other experts who study relationships say that this practical no-nonsense attitude toward marriage has become more the norm as women have piled into the workforce in recent decades. During that time, the median age of marriage has risen to 29.5 for men and 27.4 for women in 2017, up from 23 for men and 20.8 for women in 1970.

Both men and women now tend to want to advance their careers before settling down. Many are carrying student debt and worry about the high cost of housing." (Rabin, n.d.)

So now that women can have their own careers and don't need to rely on a man to support themselves, they are spending more time in the workforce and advancing their careers before getting married. If you are a successful woman who has worked your way up to a high paying, highly successful career, or if you have spent a lot of time getting a higher education, you are more likely to be single as you reach your thirties and forties.

Millennial women are also choosing to get married as a way to *enhance* their lives, not *define* them. According to an article from the Gottman Institute, women view marriage as an optional thing that happens at the right time and place in their lives.

"I'm holding off on marriage as I grow to better find my place in a world that puts women in prescriptive roles," says Nekpen Osuan, co-founder of the women's empowerment organization WomenWerk, who is 32 and plans to marry later. As she looks for the right partner to settle down with, Osuan is mindful of finding someone who shares her same values in marriage, religion, and politics. "I am navigating how *my ambition as a woman — specifically my entrepreneurial and financial goals — can fit in my goals as a future wife and mother." (Hermanson, 2018)*

According to the article, Nekpin's view on marriage is in line with the majority of Millennial women. If you spent your twenties and early thirties focusing on your career, you are well within the norm of your generation. If being single makes you feel pressured to settle down or you're getting pressure from the older generation (like a parent), your modern life is being compared to an archaic and out-dated sense of normalcy. Comparing your modern life to the lives of those in the seventies is a great way to hurt your mental health unnecessarily – and I would advise against it. Now you might be thinking but, what about loneliness? Won't I be lonely without a romantic partner?

There are many studies that prove that humans who are lonely will more likely enter depression or suffer from other mental health issues, but romantic loneliness is not the same as romantic loneliness.

A study from Harvard gives us this conclusion:

The Harvard Grant Study, one of the most comprehensive longitudinal studies on happiness, followed 268 male Harvard undergraduates for 75 years to see just what brought them joy. After nearly a lifetime of tracking, researchers discovered that fulfillment was overwhelmingly found in one thing: relationships, but not necessarily ROMANTIC relationships. (Adams, 2014)

To summarize the quote, it doesn't matter to your emotional well-being if you are single or not. Being single in and of itself does not mean you will not have the emotional support required to live a happy and healthy life.

I think this is a hugely eye-opening study. First, it tells us that no, you do not need to be in a romantic relationship in order to live a happy and fulfilled life. This is now proven by science and not something single people just say. This also means you don't need to be afraid that being single or not finding someone is going to impact your future mental health. There is no rush to settle down with someone that isn't going to be a good addition to your life. Bad and unhealthy relationships will have a much more detrimental impact on your happiness than being single.

Fully understanding this concept is the first step to finding a high-quality man because it gives you that reassurance to say "no" to anyone who doesn't bring you joy and happiness. When you reject the bad guys out there, you get one step closer to finding a good guy. If you're in a bad relationship when that good guy comes along, you blew your shot. This is why staying single can actually be the best thing you do for your future marriage.

There is also another bit of reassurance you can take away from this. If other people are pressuring you to find a partner, it's probably just because they don't know the facts. See, most people have the misconception that romantic relationships equal happiness. So, whether it's your parents or your friends who are pressuring you, they might have your best interest at heart, but they don't have the science to back themselves up. Jim Kwik, a famous author and learning expert often says, "your friends can be sincere, but they can be sincerely wrong." *& men*

"*I thought*"

The final takeaway from all of this is that if you are single and feeling down about your life, there is something deeper going on there. Depression, anxiety and other mental health issues are not caused solely by being single. Making sure that you can be happy without a romantic partner is a very important first step for dating. As a strong and independent woman, you probably have this part covered, but this is a reminder that you should not fear a future you that is single. If single you is happy right now, future single you can be happy as well.

WHAT'S THE POINT OF MARRIAGE ANYWAY?

We learned that you can survive financially when you're single and that being single doesn't negatively impact your mental health. So, then what's the point of getting married? Nowadays, although there is a tiny difference between common-law and married couples, both marriage and common-law relationships are considered "long-term" romantic relationships and are basically the same. So if I am answering the question, what's the point of marriage versus common-law? My short and to the point answer is "not much," but if we are comparing marriage and common-law relationships to being single, there's a lot more to discuss.

LONG-TERM RELATIONSHIPS vs. BEING SINGLE

Before we get into the pros and cons of these lifestyles, I really want to make it clear that a lot of the benefits of being in a long-term "forever" relationship only happen if the relationship is healthy. So the hierarchy of each life position looks like this:

Worst in every circumstance: Unhealthy relationship

Best in specific circumstances: Being Single

Best in most circumstances: Healthy relationship

When we take into account all aspects of life satisfaction (not just mental health) being in a long-term relationship *usually* comes out on top. Now before you get all down in the dumps about being single, I want to reiterate that being single versus being married shouldn't have an impact on your mental health! You can be single and be happy, you can be married and be depressed. The overall life benefits for being married have nothing to do with your day to day happiness. Now that we have that cleared up, we can look at life categories other than mental health and see how being single compares to being married.

THE TRUTHS ABOUT MONEY AND MARRIAGE

One of the more obvious benefits of getting married is the financial benefit. Even though getting married is not a financial requirement these days, it still helps to have two incomes and shared expenses. Shared housing costs, grocery bills and transportation costs are going to allow both parties to save more and invest more, therefore having an easier time building their wealth. An article comparing marriage and single life from CNN gives us the rundown:

"In their 2013 article for The Atlantic, "The High Price of Being Single in America," Lisa Arnold and Christina Campbell experimented with hypothetical single and married people's finances and discovered the marrieds came out on top over their unmarried counterparts in several key areas.

If you're single, there may be a bit less spending money, but how to spend it is your choice alone. No one can deny your dream of weekly mani-pedis or slam the door on your meticulously decorated fan cave." (Roberts, 2018)

This article is saying that if you are single, you're more likely to spend money because there's no one keeping you accountable. I think this is true only if you marry someone that isn't a big spender. The highest financial benefit will happen for you if either you or your spouse are generally smart with money. The saver usually encourages the spender to save money and together the couple expands their net worth. Another study brought to us from Money Crashers highlights another important point, however:

"A 2005 study at Ohio State University (OSU) found that after getting married, people saw a sharp increase in their level of wealth. After 10 years of marriage, the couples reported an average net worth of around $43,000, compared to $11,000 for people who had stayed single. However, people who had married and then divorced were worse off than any

other group. After a divorce, the average man was left with $8,500 in assets, while the average divorced woman had only $3,400." (Livingston, n.d.)

There it is again in black and white. If you have a healthy and happy marriage, you are more likely to increase your net worth but if your relationship is not happy and you end up getting divorced, you would have been better off staying single. Again, getting married just for the sake of getting married is detrimental to your life satisfaction. You really don't *need* a man.

I have read studies that in some cases single people can end up building a bigger net worth. This is because they often avoid expensive things like weddings or stick to buying a condo rather than a big house with expensive upkeep. Yet, it still seems like overall, married people are able to accumulate more wealth over time and more consistently. This makes sense because usually, it is two people earning money. So, if you are a person that is smart with money and you marry a spouse that is smart with money, together as a married couple you will make more money than if you stayed single. That is if you choose to get married and not have kids.

CHILDREN WILL TAKE ALL YOUR MONEY

If you are married, you are more likely to have children and that is not a good financial decision. Financially it's better if you stay single and build your wealth on your own without kids. I think this is pretty obvious so I won't spend too much time on it but I will include this excerpt from Forbes.

"Once children enter the picture, married couples are really in financial trouble: The costs to raise and educate children are staggering.

A third Chestnut client, a married couple with three children, spends $2,400 a month on food and basic household items, triple what the childless couple spends.

The total cost of camps, daycare, books, toys, and after-school programs? Try $4,000 a month. And that bill more than doubles if the kids go to private school. Families living in areas less expensive than New York City will pay less, of course, but they'll also earn less and pay a similar percentage of their income for those expenses. And all the "family discounts" in the world at ballgames, amusement parks, and museums won't put much of a dent in those bills." (Riper, 2006)

SEXUAL SATISFACTION

The research constantly proves that married couples have more frequent and higher-quality sex than single people. Although marriage has often faced the stereotype of killing sexual excitement and intimacy, the studies prove that the opposite of this is true. Statistics from Statista give us the numbers.

"71.32% of married people over 18 reported they had had sexual intercourse in the past 90 days. Only 11.32% of unattached people said they had "done the deed" during that time. (Roberts, 2018)

Married couples also have higher quality sex. Married sex is connected to feelings of love and commitment rather than just a sexual act. This can be more satisfying for both parties, but mostly for women. Women will find this kind of "committed sex" more appealing, giving women a tiny incentive to be in a long-term relationship over being single.

Married couples also have the advantage of learning about each other's sexual preferences so that they can have more satisfying and fulfilling sex compared to single people who don't usually spend many years with the same sexual partner. Having sex with the same partner also eliminates (or reduces) the fear of STI's making sex feel comfortable and stress-free. There is also a feeling of security and safety among married couples because if the couple were to get pregnant, they know that they have already committed their lives to each other. An unexpected pregnancy would be a lesser amount of stress and worry than if a single woman were to get pregnant by an <u>uncommit</u>ted partner.

Married couples also have the convenience factor working for them. They do not have to hunt for sex on dating apps or in bars, they simply have to ask their partner if they'd like to get snuggly that evening. This convenience is inevitably going to lead to more frequent sex. Although sex may seem like a minor part of the equation when we're talking about overall life satisfaction, frequent and regular sex has been surprisingly linked to <u>overall well-being</u>. See this study written in Bloom:

They found that sex enters so strongly and positively in happiness equations that they estimate that increasing intercourse from once a month to once a week is equivalent to the amount of happiness generated by adding an additional $50,000 in yearly income for the average American. They claim that the happiest folks are those getting the most sex" (Bloom, 2017)

Of course, this does depend on your natural libido and enjoyment of sex as well as the circumstances upon which you are having this sex. Generally speaking though, having more healthy, consensual and enjoyable sex is going to boost the release of feel-good hormones that will add to your overall well-being.

FREEDOM AND AUTONOMY

Here is where being single really takes the cake. If you want to live your life your way and do things the way you want, it's going to be tough to do that with another person following you around and having an opinion on all your major life decisions. I think this is a very important aspect of life to discuss because many people forget this when they enter a relationship. People want the emotional support, financial benefits and sexual satisfaction of a romantic relationship, yet they don't compromise or understand they have to take another person's opinions into account. Not understanding this key aspect to a relationship (and also to dating) is going to lead you down the path to "unhealthy relationship" which is the place we never want to go.

THE IMPORTANCE OF HEALTHY MARRIAGES

Settling down with the wrong person can be a very bad life-altering decision. All of the positive effects of marriage are washed away if the marriage is unhealthy and this can be even worse for people who are very loving and caring.

See, I'm a "relationship" person. I have always preferred to be in a long-term, committed relationship rather than being single and this has caused me to make many mistakes in the past. I would often date men who I thought were "ok" simply because I liked the idea of having a warm body next to me. It wasn't in a desperation kind of way; it was more just enjoying the feeling of being in a partnership.

I am also a good communicator and very logical thinker which made me feel that every relationship problem could just be worked through and fixed. This is not the case when you are with someone who just doesn't see life the way you do 99% of the time. No matter your social skills, communication skills and awareness of how to have a healthy relationship, if you're trying to fit a square peg in a round hole, it's just not going to work.

This is how I ended up getting myself into a completely destructive relationship that lasted three years and then another one that lasted four years. I was giving them too much "benefit of the doubt" and not listening to what I knew I needed from someone. Once I met someone who fit a lot better with my natural personality, I didn't need to know so much about conflict resolution and healthy communication because we live our day to day life in a state of happiness and only have to face conflicts every once in a while. This is the kind of relationship that you want to find, and you do this by never settling. You do this by going with your gut and listening to your instincts.

"The protective effects of marriage for physical and emotional well-being are widely documented (Carr & Springer, 2010). However, recent research shows that these effects are conditional upon the quality of the marriage; problematic marriages take an emotional toll, whereas high-quality marriages provide benefits, especially for women (Proulx, Helms, & Buehler, 2007) and older adults (Umberson, Williams, Powers, Liu, & Needham, 2006)." (Deborah Carr, 2014)

Another study highlighted by the Mental Health Foundation tells us that unhealthy relationships will impact our mental well-being and could even lead to suicidal thoughts.

"Recent studies from Ireland and the USA have found that negative social interactions and relationships, especially with partners/spouses, increase the risk of depression, anxiety, and suicidal ideation, while positive interactions reduce the risk of these issues." (Mental Health Foundation, 2013)

I don't think many of us needed a study to tell us this. If you've been in a bad relationship, you know the kind of emotional toll that it has on your daily life. In fact, experiencing this kind of emotional turmoil might leave you nervous or afraid of diving into another relationship. I know it can be hard to move on but now is a good time to remind yourself that the standards you have created for your romantic partner are essential and you must stick to knowing what you want in a man in order to lessen your chances of getting heartbroken. Even though that list of standards is just something you created on a piece of paper, I'm going to help you turn those standards into a real person.

Now that we've been through the pros and cons of being married versus being single, you can see that being single is a solid choice to live a happy and healthy life. Getting married or being in a long-term relationship has its benefits, yes, but it is important to really see what those benefits are and where you are sacrificing your freedom and autonomy for someone else. You have to decide if those sacrifices and risks are worth it for you in the long run.

Personally, I know the sacrifices I made were worth it because I wake up to my best friend every single day. I feel loved, supported and beautiful every day of my life. I know someone is there looking out for me. Someone has my back. This feeling of security and positive reassurance is worth sacrificing a bit of freedom and it's even worth risking a broken heart. I hope you feel the same way but if you don't, that's alright – you really don't need a man.

SUMMARY

In this chapter, we covered the evolution of marriage and how as a modern woman, you do not need a relationship to survive in the world. You are perfectly capable of supporting yourself. This means that marriage no longer becomes a necessity and instead, is optional. The majority of Millennials recognize this and are postponing marriage to their thirties. If you are a single Millennial, you should not feel down or upset with yourself that you haven't "found someone yet" because it's perfectly normal.

You also learned that being single in and of itself is not enough to negatively impact your mental health. If you are feeling depressed or sad about your life and you happen to be single, something else is going on with your mindset that is causing the feeling of unhappiness. It is not the fact that you are single.

We also talked about the pros and cons of marriage versus being single. This will help you decide whether the risks and rewards of a long-term relationship fit your lifestyle. There is no wrong answer here. There may be plenty of fish in the sea, but some people just don't really like fish. Or at least they don't like living with one.

CHAPTER THREE

Being Single: The Good, The Bad and Too Much Netflix

IF YOU'RE SINGLE AND IN YOUR LATE TWENTIES or older, you know you did the right thing for your overall life, but you also accidentally, set yourself up to have a very successful relationship. Even if you are not single by choice, if you are not currently in an unhealthy relationship, you increased your odds of having a future healthy relationship that will give you all the benefits we talked about earlier.

BEING SINGLE IS HELPING YOUR MARRIAGE

The interesting thing about divorce is that it has been so highly researched and studied, yet people still jump into marriage without knowing all the facts. Most of the couples I know who are married have never once looked up the rate of divorce for their demographic or the likelihood that someone in their position will get divorced. It's the blind love leading the blind. I don't want you to be one of those people, so let's have a look.

The Institute for Family Studies (Stanley, 2015) gives us the following bullet points for the traits possessed by individuals who are more likely to get divorced:

1. Marrying at a young age (e.g., marrying younger than 22)
2. Having less education (versus having a college degree)
3. Having parents who divorced or who never married
4. Having a personality that is more reactive to stress and emotion
5. Having a prior marriage that ended
6. Prior to marrying, having sex with or cohabiting with someone other than your mate

7. Having a very low income or being in poverty

Now, if you're a Millennial living in the modern world like me, your jaw might have dropped on the floor with number six. *Most* of the women in my generation have had sex or cohabitated with a man who they didn't end up marrying. Statically speaking, if you have done this, your chances of divorce have gone up but what if you had married young or skipped getting an education?

Then you would have gone from checking off one of the "divorce" boxes to checking off three -and if you check off any of the other boxes, your odds are looking worse and worse.

So just by being a Millennial, you probably *do* fit in this category:

- Prior to marrying, having sex with or cohabiting with someone other than your mate

That's one of the "divorce boxes" checked off, unfortunately, but things are looking up. Focusing on your career and education first means you likely won't fit in these categories:

- Marrying at a young age (e.g., marrying younger than 22)
- Having less education (versus having a college degree)
- Having a prior marriage that ended
- Having a very low income or being in poverty

The following category is out of your control:

- Having parents who divorced or who never married

Which this leaves us with the last one:

- Having a personality that is more reactive to stress and emotion

Now if you don't consider yourself in this category, your odds are looking really good for a healthy marriage. However, if you are a strong and independent woman who has worked your way up the career ladder, you likely *do* fit in this category. This is because just by being a woman you are biologically wired to show your emotion more than men but since that is looked down upon many professional environments, you are likely bottling up emotion that you take home with you into your personal life. The good news is, this is one of the categories you can easily control and if you do control this, you will simultaneously increase your chances of "divorce proofing" your future marriage, while also getting better at dating.

BEING SINGLE, AND BEING STRESSED

In general, women report the same causes of stress as their male counterparts. They are stressed about money, job security and health but according to the Cleveland Clinic, women are prone to higher stress because of the number of roles they tend to take on.

"Perhaps a little more unique to women are the many roles they take on. In today's society, women's roles often include family obligations, caregiving for children and/or elderly parent (statistically more likely to be a woman) and work responsibilities as well as other roles. As demands increase to fulfill these

roles, women can feel overwhelmed with time pressures and unmet obligations. They may feel a sense of failure in not being able to meet expectations for themselves and others. Oftentimes women spend more time meeting the needs of others rather than nurturing their own needs. If functioning at high-stress levels, women may not even recognize what their needs are." (Cleveland Clinic, 2019)

There are two things that are being highlighted in the above quote. The first is the idea of putting others before yourself. Even if you don't have children, your caretaker role is probably quite significant. Whether it be your friends, your parents or your siblings, there is probably a person (or people) in your life that you have chosen to put before yourself. This is one of the major reasons why women find themselves single and saying to themselves "it just kind of happened."

So much of your life revolves around other people and dating can easily fall by the wayside because it's such a solo activity. I hear this all the time from my coaching clients. I tell them to make time for going on dates throughout the week, but they insist on wanting to see their friends or their loved ones instead. This is natural.

Obviously, you want to see your friends and hang out with people you know rather than risk wasting an evening on a man that might be really boring and weird. The problem with this mindset is that the more you push off going on that date, the more days, weeks and eventually years go by without you having found a partner that you enjoy. You probably have great relationships with your friends because you have nourished those relationships, yet your dating life goes year after year without half as much attention.

The other point that was highlighted in the quote above is that women are more likely to feel stressed than men. If you're operating at a level of high stress, this can also add to the problem of not wanting to go on dates. Going out on a date has the potential to make you feel anxiety, shame and the pressure to perform, and all of these are negative emotions. The more stress and negativity that you tie to dating, the less likely you are going to want to do it.

Not only is a positive attitude key to dating, so is making sure your stress levels are managed in your day to day life. Reducing the overall stress in your life is going to help you stay positive about dating because you'll have the mental toughness and capability that you'll need to survive the tedious and frustrating endeavour that is online dating. Reducing your stress will also make you less likely to forgo the dating for more stress-relieving activities.

Let's dive into that last statement a little deeper. When you are operating at a level of high stress, you are going to be very hungry for stress relief. This means that staying home and watching Netflix is going to be a comforting activity that you gravitate towards. Being comfortable at home is the opposite of dating. Dating involves going out of your comfort zone, practicing your social skills and likely feeling rejection and shame. These are not happy emotions so you're going to run from them every chance you get. Before we move onto the next point, I want to make it very clear that doing stress-relieving activities is a good thing. You want to spend time nurturing your mental health and living a healthy single life. What you don't want to do is *avoid* your dating life because it feels uncomfortable or because it's not as comforting as your friends - or *Friends*.

THE FUTURE NEVER COMES

Many of my female clients are constantly thinking about the future. They think about the next step they want to take in their career, what life will be like when they're married or how much more they will love their lives when "X" happens. The unfortunate thing that my clients (and many women) are missing in this scenario is that happiness and a sense of life satisfaction come from *your brain*.

If you currently have a brain, then you have everything you need to see your life in a positive way. We have all heard of rich and famous people who have accomplished all their dreams yet are depressed, miserable and some have even taken their own life. We have also seen people like Stephen Hawking or Stevie Wonder overcome disabilities and challenging life circumstances in order to achieve great things and live a very fulfilling life. It is clear that wealth, fame or even circumstances don't impact our happiness. So then, what does?

The answer is something called positive psychology and this thing is amazing. Positive psychology is the study of what makes life worth living. It's the actual scientific breakdown for why we choose to get up every single morning and how we can reach the life that we picture in the future. Positive psychology says that your life is made up of a series of steps. The steps, in order, are as follows:

Step 1:   Thoughts

Step 2:   Words

Step 3:   Actions

Step 4:   Habits

Step 5:   Character

Step 5:   Your Future

Thoughts are the very first step. The thoughts that you put in your head are going to be the building blocks of your entire life. If you tell yourself that you will be happy when... then that thought gets repeated throughout your life until you die. You never actually reach the point of happiness because happiness is in your head and your head was filled with the wrong thought.

This is extremely important when it comes to dating. Many single women are so fixated on the future, that they forget to look at the present. They create fictional men in their heads and will pass up amazing partners that are right in front of them. You can't control the future, but you can control what you do right now. Remember that being stressed and being highly emotionally reactive are personality traits that increase the chances of divorce. Instead, it's better to stop fantasizing and focus on actions you can take now.

NOW IS THE TIME TO FIGURE YOURSELF OUT

When you're on the prowl for a high-quality man, it's important to take a long deep look at your current life. Are you happy where you currently live? What do you do to relax and have fun? Do you like staying put and living where you are, or do you want to travel or relocate?

What do you value most in life? Do you enjoy being close to friends and family? Do you have certain financial goals? Do you want to live in a house, apartment or a farm?

When you have concrete answers to these questions, you will start to attract a man with similar values. When you don't know where you're going or what you want out of life, you can end up with a man who doesn't share your goals. Often, women who have focused on a career and become strong and independent will start to question their lives when they hit their early thirties. This is because most women will start thinking about having a family and are not sure how that life will fit with their current lifestyle. If you have found yourself at a crossroads like this, or any other big life question, you should think about who you are and where you want to go in order to attract a man who feels the same way.

DETERMINING YOUR ATTACHMENT STYLE

Another amazing thing to do while you are single is to determine your attachment style. My coaching clients often say that knowing their attachment style is the number one thing that helped them find successful relationships.

According to psychologists Bartholomew and Horowitz, there are four attachment styles that determine the way we behave in relationships. Your attachment style mostly comes from what you experienced as a child, but experiences can change this over time. This means that you can start off having one attachment style but then a boyfriend or other loving relationship could change your style for better or for worse. Here are the four attachment styles.

SECURE

The secure attachment style is best defined by the abilities to not fear the future and to be able to move on from the past. People with secure attachment styles are not afraid of their hearts being broken. They are not afraid to take this risk and if they do get their heart broken, they can grieve, mourn the loss and healthily enter a new relationship. People with this style also do not fear intimacy or closeness. They do not pull back when someone shows signs of intimacy or connection in order to protect themselves. They are not afraid of depending on others. They understand that loving relationships involve give and take and they are ok with both of those things. They do not worry about being abandoned or left behind.

ANXIOUS

The anxious attachment style is best defined by someone who is afraid that they're going to be abandoned. This often makes them clingy and needy which ironically makes others pull away and not want to be with them. Anxious people can be jealous, possessive and feel the need for constant reassurance. They often need validation that the other person still loves them. Relationships with an anxious person will often be filled with drama or issues that need to be sorted out on a regular basis.

AVOIDANT

People who have this attachment style are independent and do not want to be tied down by another person.

They need space, like to have control and like to be the one to fuel the decision making. They tend to focus on their personal lives more than creating strong emotional bonds with others. They find it difficult to give in and depend or "need" someone else. They have a hard time trusting. They also view themselves highly and don't struggle with self-esteem or confidence issues. They can sometimes be narcissistic.

FEARFUL

People with this attachment style combine the traits of anxious and avoidant. They have high anxiety; they fear rejection or being left alone. Rather than become clingy like the anxious style, they withdraw and pull back as a way to cope. This kind of attachment style has a lot of highs and lows. They want to get close but then pull back when they feel they might be getting too close that they may get hurt. This attachment style is often a result of past trauma, emotional abuse or mental health issues like anxiety or depression.

Knowing what attachment style you have can work wonders on your feelings and behavior while dating.

Are you feeling the overwhelming need to text him and check-in? You might have an anxious attachment style. Do you feel suffocated or a loss of control in your life if you get too close to someone? You might have an avoidant attachment style.

The best way to cope with this is to remember that these attachment styles have been ingrained into your personal being for many years. They are part of you, and instead of trying to fight them, it's best to find healthy ways to cope and overcome them. You can do this by speaking with a coach or researching your personal attachment style and finding resources that will help you get closer to "secure" attachment.

IN SUMMARY

Being single is a mish-mash of different things happening all at once. You want to live a healthy happy life by spending time with your friends, pursuing your hobbies and finding ways to relax, but you also want to make dating a priority and avoid it falling by the wayside just because it's not fun. The grass is greener where you water it, so avoiding dating so you can stay in your comfort zone will definitely hurt your chances of finding a high-quality man.

You also want to figure yourself out and pinpoint exactly what you want out of a relationship. This will help you find someone who is in line with your goals and thus will have long-term potential. Finally, you want to determine your attachment style so that you can work on healthy ways of coping and increase your chances of finding a partner that is secure and mentally healthy. Your head needs to be in the right place if you want to find a good partner. We'll be tackling more of that in the next chapter.

CHAPTER FOUR

The Dating Lens and The Mindset of Success

"BELIEVE IT CAN BE DONE, WHEN YOU BELIEVE something can be done, really believe, your mind will find the ways to do it. Believing in solution paves the way to solution." (Schwartz, 1959)

This is a quote from a very popular book called "The Magic of Thinking Big". Is it cheesy? Yes, but I think your thoughts play a huge role in your life's outcomes. You need to get your brain on your side. Your brain can either build you up and take you exactly where you want to go, or it can strip everything away from you and keep you living the worst life in the world.

CHANGING YOUR PERSPECTIVE

Another way to describe this is to use the word perspective. Perspective is the *way you see things*. Let's use a quick example. Imagine you and your kids are at home when suddenly you feel shaking. There is a huge earthquake happening and your whole house is shaking from side to side. Although it felt like an hour, once the two-minute earthquake is finished, you take a look around. To your horror, everything is destroyed. The roof has caved in, the walls are barely holding together and there's not a single possession in the house worth saving. After you see what has happened to your house, you can't help but feel like the luckiest person on earth.

You and your children have all managed to get through this, injury-free. Despite having everything you own completely destroyed. The perspective that you have in this situation is nothing but pure joy and gratitude. It could have been so much *worse*.

On the outside, this situation is truly horrible. Imagine calling a friend to tell her your whole house and all your possessions have been destroyed in an earthquake. She would probably feel very sad for you. She might cry or tell you how sorry she is that this happened, but you wouldn't need much pity or sympathy. You consider this the luckiest day of your life. The "lens" through which she views this situation is much different than your lens. You're just seeing your children, happy, healthy and un-harmed. This "lens" is the perspective that you see the world and it comes up every single day of your life.

Are you upset that your coffee is too strong, or are you happy to have some caffeine to get you through Monday? Are you upset that your car won't start or are you happy that jumpstarting your battery is a pretty low cost, low time commitment repair? Are you upset that your child got an F in school or are you happy that he is now asking you for help? This "lens" also applies to dating. We can call it your "dating lens".

When you have been dating for a while and nothing has come of it, it is very easy to let your dating lens get bitter and jaded. Swipe after swipe, message after message and bad date after bad date. Nothing is coming of this. The more jaded and bitter you allow yourself to get with the process, the more likely you are to give up completely. If you take anything away from this book it should be this: *the feelings associated with endless dating have no similarities to the feelings felt in a healthy relationship.* Let me elaborate.

You know how dating can make you feel sad, tired and like no one is going to be a good fit for your life? Well, being in a healthy relationship makes you feel the opposite. It gives you a support system, lifts you up when you're down and reminds you every day that you have found someone to tackle life's problems with. When you look at it this way, the frustrations of dating seem much more worth it.

When you're getting jaded and bitter at the dating process, you might say "I'm done with this whole dating thing" but you're throwing away the baby with the bathwater if you give up. Dating (especially online dating) isn't all that fun, but it's a means to an end. An end filled with a lot of positivity. You need to constantly remind yourself of this. You do this by taking care of your dating lens. Taking good care of your lens is one of the most important things you'll do for your dating life, but also your life in general.

Early in my coaching career, I saw how important the dating lens was when working with a client named Rhonda. Rhonda was an extremely anxious person, and when I first talked to her on the phone, I almost didn't want to take her on as a client. She was very negative and talked a lot about how she doesn't deserve a good relationship and that online dating is the pit of hell. After working with Rhonda for a few weeks, nothing had changed, she was still bitter and anxious about the entire process. Feeling worried as a young coach, with a client I thought I wouldn't be able to help, I knew I had to think outside of the box.

On our next coaching call, I told Rhonda that I had a challenge for her. I wanted her to forget about dating. Forget about finding "the one" on these apps and instead, I challenged her to find a friend. The only conditions for this friend were that he had to be male and she had to meet him from one of the dating apps or sites. I told her that I would not let her schedule another call with me until she had found a friend from one of the dating apps.

So off she went for a few weeks, and then one day I got an email from her. "I found a friend," she said, "can we schedule a call?" On our call, she told me that she had gone out with a man thinking and knowing that he would just be a friend. All the pressure was off. She relaxed, calmed down and actually enjoyed herself on the date. She went on another date with another man and again, she felt calm and collected while talking to him. Neither of these "friends" ended up working out but something in Rhonda had completely changed. Once all the pressure was removed from dating, it was much easier to do. She told me on the phone that when she went out with men thinking that they would only be friends, she could see dating for what it really is.

"You're not getting married," I told her, "It's just drinks."

After that, her mentality completely changed and she was able to find a little more joy out of dating. Her calls with me after that were much more positive and optimistic.

I know dating can be frustrating, but your life demands that you take on much more challenging and stressful situations. Going for drinks or dinner once a week is not as bad as our brains make it out to be. No, I'm not trying to make light of your emotions, I'm just trying to help you clean up that dating lens.

USING YOUR DATING LENS TO FACE REJECTION

No matter how much you try to improve your dating skills and become the best version of yourself, you're still going to get rejected. Depending on how you felt about the person who is rejecting you, it's either going to hurt a little or hurt a lot, but rejection is nearly always going to hurt. Rather than letting this inevitable part of dating start corrupting your dating lens, it's best to learn how to accept rejection and keep trying.

Let's take a look at Stephen King. Stephen King, as we know him now, is one of the best and most successful authors of all time. When he was pitching his first book, "Carrie" to publishers, he was rejected thirty times. Let's pause here for a moment and think about this. The best fiction writer in the world was rejected by *thirty* publishers. It is a publisher's sole purpose of existing to read a manuscript and decide if it will be good enough to sell to an audience. How is it that thirty of them got this so wrong? The answer is made up of a million different reasons but let's cover a few of them:

1. They didn't read the manuscript
2. They didn't want to give a new writer a chance
3. They didn't like the book
4. They didn't like Stephen King's photo
5. They didn't realize millions of people *would* like it.

Notice the general trend these reasons follow? They all have to do with the publishers, and nothing to do with Stephen King. None of the rejections had anything to do with King's talent as a writer, and everything to do with the mistakes, ignorance, and opinion of the publishers. Now let's look at swiping on Tinder.

When you are swiping or messaging candidates on a dating site, these candidates are much like the publishers in the above scenario. Although they may reject you, ghost you or stand you up on a date, this has nothing to do with *you* and everything to do with *them*. The first lesson to take away here is this:

If you keep your dating lens positive and optimistic, rejection may hurt, but it will not make you stop trying.

Your dating lens should be kept squeaky clean no matter what happens. You must clean up any spots that are going to make you see the world in a negative way. The way you do this is by working on your self-love, your inner dialogue, and your mental health. We will be discussing this in more detail throughout this book.

THE POWER OF PERSISTENCE

The other lesson to be learned from Stephen King's story is that of persistence. The ability to keep trying. When Stephen King had been rejected for the thirtieth time, he threw his manuscript for "Carrie" in the trash. He was done. Too many rejections. Luckily for us book lovers, King's wife pulled the manuscript out of the garbage and encouraged him to keep trying. You see, the biggest way to stop yourself from achieving a goal is to stop trying to get it. Had Stephen King given up then and there, he would have forever lived his life as a failed writer. A writer that didn't make it.

You could also take these statistics as motivation to keep you swiping:

"Over 44 percent of women and 38.4 percent of men are looking for serious, long-term relationships when using a dating [site or app]—that's a huge difference from only 22.6 percent of men and 14.8 percent of women who are looking for something more casual." (Jessee, n.d.)

See! Most people are looking for real love.

Sometimes the only limitations that really impact us are the ones we put on ourselves. Many times, a coaching client will say to me on the phone "I'm never going to find someone" and I often say to them "You're right, you probably won't". If you don't think you can do it, you probably can't. So, the very first step that you have to take is you need to believe in yourself. Believe in your ability to find someone who loves you for who you are. Believe that yes, despite your flaws, you *deserve* love. You are worthy of it. The man for you is out there and he wants to be that person for you. You just have to keep trying to find him.

NATALIE AND THE CHEATING EX

Now is a good time to talk about one of my favorite clients, her name was Natalie. Natalie was a thirty-five-year-old pediatrician. She worked long hours and had spent a lot of years in medical school. She eventually found herself single in her thirties and wanted to settle down. Natalie definitely believed in her ability to find a high-quality partner; she had no problem with that. She was very confident, assertive, and she went out of her way to make herself feel attractive. She loved designer clothing and buying very expensive makeup. She was a very attractive woman that could easily find any man, yet I was able to understand why no man was interested in her after she told me just one story. A story of a date she went on.

After a few days on Bumble, Natalie had a date set up with a friendly man who was very attractive. They met at a coffee shop near his office and started getting to know each other. Natalie was excited about him and could really see herself continuing to see this man.

After they had been talking to each other for about an hour, she asked him a very serious question.

"Do you think it's ok to cheat on someone?" She asked.

Not wanting to be rude, and genuinely interested in the conversation up until that point, the man answered, "No, I don't think that's ok, in fact, I have been cheated on in the past".

What started out as a light-hearted and fun date quickly turned awkward. While someone quick on their feet might have been able to turn the conversation around, Natalie was not very outgoing and couldn't easily recover. She got flustered and awkward and the mood was killed for the rest of the date. I'm not sure what she was thinking when she asked this question if she wasn't ready to hear the answer. I think she just got ahead of herself and made a mistake. Regardless, he never reached out to her for a second date.

There is a lot to look at when analyzing the above scenario. If they had been truly hitting it off, it's hard to believe that one little comment like that could really set the whole date on a downward spiral. Yet, I do strongly believe that Natalie misstepped a couple of times here.

HUMANS NEED TO START SMALL

First of all, she shouldn't have asked such a personal question on the first date. See, humans are hardwired to protect themselves from emotional vulnerability because they naturally fear rejection. We are tribal animals and not fitting in with the tribe could cost us our lives. This is why most of us won't reveal our true selves until we know it's safe. We also look differently upon people who *do* reveal themselves too quickly. They're either extremely brave or ridiculously stupid. Most humans hardwired to start with small talk before proceeding to deeper conversations. Small talk exists because we don't want to open our vulnerabilities and insecurities to just any human. This is why a first date conversation should be kept lighthearted and fun. You're not trying to find out the other person's deepest darkest secrets, you're just trying to create a safe space so that these secrets can be revealed later. The first date is about creating that safe environment. What Natalie did with her question was she tried to pull out a vulnerability from her date even though he might not have been ready to share it. Then, she was awkward about his answer which probably made him feel rejected. This made the connection between the two of them decrease instead of increase. This not good for trying to get to date number two. So, Natalie made a serious mistake here but, to my surprise, she wouldn't admit it.

THE GROWTH MINDSET

"He became super moody after I asked him that and I don't think I want to date a man who can't handle a deeper conversation", She told me.

Natalie was missing a key component of the success mindset which is, *always look to grow*. Growth is something that successful people do. They look at situations and they think to themselves, how could this have gone better? What can I do to improve next time? When you look at bad dates with this positive dating lens, you can never really go on a bad date because every date is a chance to grow. Dates are a chance to work on your social skills, your conversational skills and your ability to think on your toes. Every date comes with a lesson. It's up to you (or your dating coach) to help you find out what is to be learned so that you can improve next time.

Taking this approach to dating is something most people never do. They go on a date, it goes wrong and they never take another second to think about it. This is wrong. Remember what I said earlier in this book that dating is a set of skills. Each skill can be worked on, practiced and improved upon. It's important to remember this because most people who are not paying attention won't improve their dating ability as they go on more dates. Someone who has been single for years may have never taken the time to look inward and see what they could have been doing differently to reach better results.

A BRIEF LOOK AT EMOTIONAL INTELLIGENCE

The other thing that Natalie mentioned was that "he got moody" after she asked him the question. If he got moody, that means he was having an emotional reaction to something that Natalie had said. If Natalie was a little better at reading his body language and social cues, she would have apologized. She would have told him that she didn't mean to hit a sore spot and that they could talk about that another time if he wished. Saying something like this would have shown a lot of maturity and *emotional intelligence.*

Emotional Intelligence is a very important thing to have in life, but especially in dating. Emotional intelligence, sometimes referred to as EQ is when someone has the ability to identify and manage one's own emotions as well as the emotions of others. Let's break this down further.

Identifying someone's emotions means that you can guess via their body language, tone of voice and choice of words how they might be feeling. If someone says "oh no, that's alright, I'm fine" but their lip is quivering and their voice is shaking, they might be on the verge of tears. Being able to identify what's really going on with someone is part of EQ. It's looking at subtleties to try and get an idea of what they're feeling inside.

The other part of EQ is the ability to *manage* either your emotions or the emotions of others. In the story above, Natalie was able to identify the man's emotions really well. She was able to see that he got quiet and moody after she asked him a question and she realized it wouldn't be a good call to push him and make him talk about the topic in more detail. Unfortunately, Natalie missed the "managing emotions" part because she made no effort to take him out of the mood she put him in and guide his emotion to a happier place. She was also unable to manage her own emotion. She clearly got upset after he took the question the wrong way and wasn't able to change her attitude and her mood in order to save the date.

Wow, Natalie had a lot to learn, didn't she? See, something as simple as Natalie's story is filled with many lessons that can improve your dating abilities, however, the biggest lesson during this whole experience was a lesson for me.

NATALIE OR SAMANTHA

After I explained to Natalie everything about emotional intelligence and humans needing to go slow before they can truly connect, to my surprise, she disagreed with me. She told me that she didn't think the question was such a big deal and that I was blowing it out of proportion. This was a big lesson for me. I learned that not everybody is ready to accept help. Some people might think they want to change the outcomes of their life, but if they're not ready to accept a helping hand, they will never change anything. If you don't have the "success mindset" locked down, anything I try to teach you will be ignored and therefore wasted. This is why adopting a "growth" mindset is key to your success on the dating scene. You must be willing to admit to yourself that what you have done in the past has not worked and you might be able to learn something new.

Do you remember the story of Samantha and the coal miner? There is a very good reason why I chose to start my book with that story. There are many "Samanthas" in the world - and some of them are named Natalie. Natalie chose to ignore my advice on the situation. She preferred to walk through the coal mine without a hard hat. Something that Natalie doesn't realize is that her attitude toward this situation is actually setting her up for a future failed or unhealthy relationship. See, Natalie's lack of ability to look inward is one of the most common ways that people sabotage their relationships. John Gottman, who is a well-known marriage and relationship researcher said the following in an interview about being able to predict divorce:

"We can predict divorce and red flags in a couple's relationship from just the first three minutes of how they talk about an area of disagreement. Just the way they bring up the issue...the ones who are not going to work out are the ones who bring up the issue as though their partner's character is defective...they're really in this attack mode...you know the problem is really you, you need to change your personality, you need therapy." (Gottman, 2010)

Gottman is saying that if you paint the other person to be the enemy, there is no way to move forward in a healthy way with that person. Some of you might think that this doesn't really apply to dating, but you're missing the mark. Learning how to be a more effective dater is going to teach you the same skills you need to be a better girlfriend. It's teaching you how to see the world from someone else's point of view.

Oftentimes, single people get so caught up in their own lives that they forget what it's like to see things through the eyes of their partner. This is because single people don't need the approval of others on a daily basis. If you are single and you want Thai food for dinner, you get it. If you want to watch *Friends* on Netflix, you do it. Dating is the very first step to letting someone else into your life and understanding that now there are two people involved in making decisions. If a man you're seeing chooses to talk about his job all night, that was his choice and it's up to you decide if you want to work with him to be a better listener or if you would rather start a clean slate with someone else. Either way, dating involves thinking about others and *really and truly* understanding that not everyone is going to see things the way you do.

THE COMPONENTS OF THE SUCCESS MINDSET

In this chapter, we talked about the success mindset, how it's going to impact the way you learn about dating and the way you approach dating moving forward. You learned that your perspective or your "dating lens" needs to stay positive and optimistic in order for you to be successful. Dating is a big undertaking that involves a lot of emotional drain. With your "dating lens" clean and ready to handle the toughest challenges, you will be set up for success in this area. Now don't worry about *how* to keep your dating lens optimistic and positive, we will be discussing that later. For now, all you need to know is that you must have a dating lens and that you must take care of it.

You also learned about persistence. The ability to keep moving forward despite rejection. Humans fear rejection because we are tribal animals. This makes it very easy to give in and give up at the first sign of rejection. Remember Stephen King. Rejection has nothing to do with you and everything to do with the person rejecting you. It is also inevitable, meaning you will never put yourself out there and be accepted one hundred percent of the time. So, if you're not batting those odds, don't beat yourself up about it.

The final component of a success mindset is having the ability to grow. The growth mindset is what keeps you humble. It allows you to learn and improve every step of the way. Fighting the success mindset and failure to look inward will have you walking through a coal mine without any protection. You'll have a very dirty and negative dating lens. When you accept that you might not have all the answers and are willing to have someone else tell you them, your high-quality man will seem to have just appeared at your doorstep. This chapter covered a lot about mindset, but it's not so easy to just "think positively" is it? Let's take a look at that.

CHAPTER FIVE

The Emotions of Dating

IF YOU'RE GOING ON A TRIP, LET'S SAY A FISHING trip, it helps to be prepared. You need the right gear, the right location, and the proper knowledge to make your trip successful. This logic applies to nearly everything we do and it even applies to dating. One thing that will help you greatly while you're dating is to understand and learn how to deal with the emotions that you'll inevitably face.

Now let me ask you a very important question. Where did you learn how to date? People who like to ski, fish, play the piano or do any kind of activity usually learned it from somewhere. Whether it was a teacher, a parent or a book. Although this is the route most of us take with our hobbies, interests, and careers, very few of us actually make the extra effort to learn about dating and relationships. Most of us haven't taken the effort to learn from someone who was qualified and educated in this field. We simply learned by doing what our friends did or asking our parents or siblings. It's important to remember that the bad habits you have likely picked up along the way don't have to be part of you forever. You can change your mindset and approach to something that is much more effective. Although it's difficult to stay level-headed when dealing with such an emotionally charged thing as dating, it can be extremely helpful. Let's take a look at the emotions of dating and apply some logic to them.

VULNERABILITY

I decided not to start this chapter slowly. I wanted to jump in and get right to the good stuff. The real meat of human connection and the emotion that we must be willing to feel in order to be successful at finding a high-quality partner. If you have been burned in the past or feel any kind of insecurity when it comes to finding a romantic partner, you are likely afraid to be vulnerable. You probably have a wall up that is there to protect yourself from getting hurt. It's there to stop your heart from being broken. Does a heart ever truly heal after being broken? Are you ever able to love the same way you did when you were experiencing it for the first time? I don't think anyone can really know if a heart can be fully healed, but we have to try our best to get it as close as possible to the state it was in before it got broken. This state of fearlessness is your key to success.

When people have been in very bad relationships that ended in heartbreak, they start to associate love with pain. They find themselves searching for love with one foot out the door because they are thinking to themselves, how do I avoid pain? How do I stop myself from getting hurt? So, the wall goes up.

Let me ask you something. What is this wall actually doing? Is it protecting you from harm? Stopping all the bad guys from getting in? What else is it stopping from getting in? Let's just give the wall the benefit of the doubt for a moment. Let's say that the wall is working and is stopping the bad guys from getting in. The problem here is that the wall blocks what is coming in but also what is going out. You're not able to *give* if you have this wall up. You can't share your full self and be *vulnerable* without risking getting your heartbroken.

Let's break this down a little more. You have your wall up and you are feeling quite good about yourself. Yet, you find that you can't really show the other person how much they mean to you without revealing your true feelings.

Saying "I like you" takes the wall down.

Saying "I need you" takes the wall down.

If you put your feelings and your heart on the other side of the wall, they are no longer protected. Can someone really love you if you're not sharing your full self with them? In short, the answer is no.

Keeping your heart on the safe side of the wall means that you are not being vulnerable. The definition of being vulnerable is that you are susceptible to physical or emotional harm. This seems like a stupid position to put yourself in, but this is actually how humans connect with each other.

Brene Brown, a well-renowned researcher talked about the importance of vulnerability in human connection in her Ted Talk called "The Power of Vulnerability" (Brown, 2010). She breaks the steps down as follows:

1. The point of human existence is a connection with others.
2. Shame is the fear of disconnection from others.
3. Vulnerability is the act of showing our true selves to others.
4. Connection is when our true selves are accepted by others.

You can see that she has created a step by step ladder to establish a true connection with others and it all starts with being vulnerable. Let's use an example of this so you can see how it really makes sense.

Imagine it's your first day at work at a very high paying job. You really want to fit in and you see a group of your co-workers sitting at a table having lunch. You go over and you overhear them all speaking badly about Star Wars, saying that it's a dumb movie. Star Wars is your favorite movie, you've loved it since you were a kid. Now let's imagine you say to them "yeah, I hate Star Wars too, it's so nerdy." If they all agree with you and invite you to sit with them, you may be "part of the group" but you know deep down that this is not a real connection. They are not accepting the real you.

On the flip side, if you didn't lie to them and told them the truth, that you like Star Wars, the situation could play out in one of two ways. They will either laugh and make fun of you and not invite you to sit with them (rejection), or they might say "hey, that's cool" and invite you to sit with them anyway (acceptance).

As you can see, revealing your true self poses a bit of a risk. You will either face acceptance or rejection. In the dating world, trying to "fit in" or protect yourself from rejection by not revealing your true feelings might stop you from getting hurt, but it will also stop you from ever finding real love.

REJECTION

Rejection or feeling rejected is another emotion that comes along with dating. As I mentioned earlier, if we reveal our true selves to others, we are going to get rejected a few times. It's just part of living in a world with 7 billion different personalities. In order to date successfully, we have to let go of the fear of rejection. Most of us have this fear of rejection, or fear of pain because we have been through heartache or bad breakups in the past. Going through a bad break up is one of the most difficult emotional pains that a human can go through. It is rejection by someone to whom you revealed your whole true self.

Although this pain can be unbearable, overcoming it and letting your wall down is essential to finding new love. The good news is there are ways to get rid of this fear and deal with rejections.

The first step is understanding that shame is universal. Remember, shame is the fear of disconnection with others. This is what stops us from being vulnerable. Brene Brown found in her research that nearly all humans feel shame. The only ones who don't are the "people who don't have the capacity for human empathy or connection." (Brown, 2010)

This includes people who have mental disabilities so severe they are incapable of feeling love. So, unless you are in a coma or have a severe mental disability, you will be faced with feeling shame at one point or another. If you think it's hard to reveal your true feelings or that it's hard to open up to others, I have good news, it means you're a normal functioning human.

An excellent way to overcome the fear of rejection is to build a solid foundation within yourself. Let's imagine you have a house made of straw. Your straw house is not very strong, so you build up a big wall around it so that nothing can get near it. The problem is that the first thing to get over the wall is going to take the whole house down. It's not a good long-term strategy. Instead, build a brick house so that you don't even need a wall – you know you're safe even though you're fully exposing yourself to anything that might attack you.

TRUST

Is trust an emotion? I'm not sure but I needed to put it in here. When you're trying to find a romantic partner, you must have the ability to trust others.

"The only way to know if you can trust somebody is to trust them." ~Ernest Hemmingway

The people who are deserving of your trust are the people who have it and don't abuse it. There is not a single way of knowing if someone is going to abuse it unless you give them a chance. Trust is given and measured on an individual basis. If your friend's mom breaks your trust, it doesn't mean *all moms* are not trustworthy. If a man breaks your trust, it doesn't mean all men are not trustworthy. Generalizations don't work well when we are dealing with people. Every situation lives in its own set of circumstances. Everyone is different.

Trust plays a huge role in the dating world because you need to believe that people have good intentions and are trying their best. I have a client who is currently seeing a very nice guy. He is a little nerdy and definitely awkward, much like her and they seem to get along well. After they had their second date, she called me up and told me that she wasn't interested in him anymore, so I asked her why. She told me that he didn't offer to pay for the dinner or the movie they went to. She was totally turned off by this lack of chivalry and was ready to call it quits.

Let's go back to "trust". We have to trust that people are not doing things to intentionally hurt us. Now don't get me wrong, I am not saying that you should let things slide if they are truly deal-breakers that you can't stand, but my client in this situation really liked this man. She was attracted to him, he had a good job, they got along very well and he would make her laugh. In a situation like this, you have to weigh the pros and cons and trust that maybe he just made an innocent mistake. Maybe he just got nervous and blurted out "separate" checks when the waiter went by. Whatever the reason, it's best for her to trust that he's interested in her and is trying his best.

I chose this light-hearted example to show you that trust is necessary for the big things, like trusting that he isn't sleeping with other women and also the little things like he didn't pay because he didn't know it was romantic versus he didn't pay because he's not taking you seriously.

You might be thinking that someone needs to earn your trust, but it's actually the opposite. Trust should be fully given until the other person has given you a reason to take it away. Innocent until proven guilty.

OVERTHINKING

This is the big one. Most of my coaching clients face this problem in their personal lives as well as their dating lives. The feeling of thoughts racing through your head and making mountains out of molehills. This is something that many successful women go through. Overthinking seems to be a by-product of being organized, structured and successful, but don't worry there are ways to curb it.

How is it that successful people can have thriving friendships, relationships with their siblings and parents, but struggle significantly when it comes to romantic relationships? Well, I think we can blame Hollywood for that one. It's true! You've probably grown up with the idea that romantic relationships are somehow better or more exciting than regular old friendships, but they're really not. A relationship is pretty much just a friendship.

Now don't get me wrong, I don't want to downplay this too much because you're going to spend a lot more time with your significant other than you would with your friends. I'm just saying that the skills you have that make you a good friend, are the same skills that are going to make you a good romantic partner.

Most of the time we are quick to forgive our friends and give them benefit of the doubt. Do you have a friend that annoys you sometimes? Maybe she talks too much about herself, maybe she cancels your plans last minute or she always shows up late. We all have friends and family members that are annoying in their own way, yet we still love them.

When it comes to romantic relationships, people can be so quick to overthink and analyze every little detail about the other person. When your brain gets into a cycle of overthinking, this will quickly lead to stress and anxiety. Having dating be so emotionally charged with negative emotions (stress, anxiety and overthinking) is going to make it difficult to see the positive in dating and it's going to make you want to give up. It can also make you sabotage a good relationship with a high-quality man.

The absolute best way to be successful at dating is to get a better handle at controlling your thoughts. Your brain needs to help you get through this. It needs to be your biggest support system. It cannot be the cause of your anxiety and stress while you're doing something that is already a very highly emotional experience.

One way you can control your thoughts is by learning the most basic aspects of cognitive-behavioral therapy, or CBT. CBT just means learning how to control your thoughts. The first step is that your brain has two types of thoughts. First, you have automatic thoughts. These thoughts are the ones that just pop into your head. You don't control them. If these thoughts tend to be negative or anxiety-inducing, it's going to benefit you to change them. The problem is, you can't just directly change automatic thoughts, it doesn't work that way. The way you start to change those thoughts is by focusing on your "controllable thoughts" these are the ones you *do* control.

It's easy to control a controllable thought. I can make you do it right now by telling you to picture a green dragon breathing fire into the sky. Can you picture that green dragon? Sure, you can. That's a controllable thought. Our goal is to make our controllable thoughts positive and supportive.

Thoughts like: "I can never succeed," or "just my luck," are unhelpful and often pop into our heads without our permission. These negative predictions weaken your will power and make it difficult for you to have a positive perspective on any of your life situations. You must learn to replace such unhelpful thoughts with realistic statements. When you think "I will never find true love," replace it with a positive thought that you control. Something like: "I have distinct virtues that a man will appreciate."

Research has proven that our brains lie to us, (Wang, 2008). When it tells you that dating sucks or that there's no man out there for you, consider it a challenge. Whenever you feel you cannot keep going, strive to do something that you don't want to do. Go on a date that you felt like canceling, give a man you didn't like a second chance. Every time you succeed in proving your brain wrong, the brain will see you in a different light. This will allow you to consider limitations and your capacity from another angle.

Be aware of the negative thought patterns that paralyze you. Identify these patterns and develop a personal mantra to counter whatever negativity with which you are confronted. Hence, repeat things like "It won't matter in the long run," or "I've got this" disarms the negativity, and, with time, your subconscious will believe and accept these affirmations as valid, in contrast with the unhealthy things you were once used to.

Training the brain to think in a different and positive way is like building a new skill. It takes time and consistency to build. However, constant practice and consistency will slowly build up your mental muscle.

INSECURITY & LACK OF CONFIDENCE

This is a dating emotion that I find comes in waves with a lot of my clients. My clients tend to be very successful women who have established themselves in many areas of their lives, so they do feel generally confident about themselves and what they have achieved. That being said, we all face moments of self-doubt or low self-confidence. Some people may experience this more than others, but all of us will have a "low self-esteem'" day or two in our lives.

Low self-esteem can be triggered by dating because it's such a personally revealing endeavor. It involves finding someone that must like every aspect of you and your personality. They have to like your values, some of your hobbies, your sense of humor, where you live, your appearance and more. Humans are social creatures; we really want to be accepted by others and when we're not accepted it really hurts. As I mentioned when speaking about vulnerability, humans hate rejection and if we face rejection a few too many times, we are going to start critiquing ourselves and making ourselves more insecure.

Just like most personality traits, confidence comes from within. It is a mental state. When you achieve true confidence, not only are you going to look more attractive and appealing to others, you are going to feel secure and attractive within yourself.

Confidence involves two different parts and our goal to achieve better confidence is to make sure we have both parts lined up. The first part is "inner confidence" this involves the actual feelings we have about ourselves inside, also known as self-esteem. You could be the most powerful and outspoken woman in a room, but if you go home at night and overly critique yourself and are plagued with insecurities, you have outside confidence but not inner confidence.

Inner confidence is the most important step because without it, even if you have good social skills, you will always have this feeling that you're faking it or that you're not good enough. One of the easiest ways to start achieving inner self-confidence is to stop judging yourself and others.

People who suffer from low self-esteem are often very self-aware. They look inward to see how they can improve and how they are coming across to others. They do this with other people too. They see it when someone is shy or nervous or saying the wrong things, and they make a mental note of it. Whenever you judge others, you create an idea in your head that other people are doing the same thing. If you laugh at a woman for not wearing any makeup at the club, you are creating the idea in your head that other people will laugh at you if you don't wear makeup in the club.

This judgment of others is going to really backfire on your self-confidence because your brain knows all of your deepest insecurities. Let's say that you feel a little insecure about your acne. Then a woman walks into the room and she has worse acne than you. You're probably going to think, wow that woman has some serious acne, that's so gross! And although that thought seemed harmless, you basically told yourself that having acne looks gross, when you have it as well. Because your brain knows all of your sore spots, it's going to be easy for it to pinpoint and judge those same spots in others, thus destroying your confidence.

Creating a judgemental world in your head makes you feel afraid. It makes you afraid to put yourself out there and not care about what people think. So, step number one in achieving better confidence is to stop judging others.

Not judging others will help boost your confidence and will make you easier going when it comes to dating. My clients will often tell me the tiniest little things that they observed about their date. "He wore hiking shoes to dinner" or "he was really nervous and didn't look me in the eye." These are little tiny things that you're picking on and you are judging the person because of them. You are thinking to yourself "this guy doesn't have a good fashion sense" or "this guy is an awkward nerd."

Judging people is when you observe something in someone else and you draw up your own conclusion of them. You put labels or stereotypes on that person because of something they said or did. Let's take the previous example of hiking shoes at dinner. If you saw that and you were judging the person for it, you might draw up the following conclusions:

- He doesn't have a good fashion sense
- He's lazy and doesn't care about our date

- He's low-class

Any one of these conclusions may be true or they may be false, but none of them tell you what kind of boyfriend he's going to be. If he has good communication skills, is funny and accepts you for who you are, surely, he might be able to wear a different pair of shoes if you asked him nicely. This example may seem ridiculous and petty, but you'd be surprised at how many of my clients judge men for these kinds of things. Before we move on, let's just be very clear here. The point of this example is not that you should cut men slack and date them if they do something that you don't like, it's that you shouldn't be judging them in the first place because this is going to help your self-confidence.

Another way to boost your self-confidence is to use the CBT methods that we spoke about earlier. Your brain should be your biggest fan, your loudest cheerleader. When you use positive controllable thoughts to change your negative automatic thoughts, you are creating a safe and supportive environment in your brain. If you stop judging others and remind yourself to think supportive and positive thoughts, you will be well on your way to real self-confidence.

SMALL TALK

The other part of confidence is "outer confidence". This is the part that involves showing other people that you are secure within yourself and that you have good social skills. One thing to remember is that your confidence level can change depending on the situation. A powerful CEO who is confident and outspoken could be shy or intimidated on a date with a handsome man. In order to have true confidence, your social skills should be the same no matter the situation.

One way that you can have more self-confidence is by mastering your small talk skills. Many people tell me that they don't like to engage in small talk. Instead, they prefer deeper and more meaningful conversations. Well, guess what? Everyone feels this way! Nobody wants to talk about the weather or what they had for lunch. We would all prefer to engage in a hilarious conversation about our favorite TV show or some juicy gossip about a co-worker. Small talk is boring and yet, it is essential. So, even if you are naturally good at small talk and are very outgoing, you will find it beneficial to understand the role it's actually playing in meeting new people. Remember Natalie from earlier in this book? She wasn't able to create a safe environment for her date which was a huge mistake.

As we learned from Natalie's story, the best small talk is positive and light-hearted and shows that you are accepting the other person. If they say, "aw man I have such a big project coming up" you don't want to say "ouch, you're probably never going to get it done" because that is telling them you are negative, you don't have faith in their abilities and you don't have any helpful solutions. The space you just created here is full of negativity and so they are going to be less eager to open up to you and reveal more of themselves to you.

One way you can create a safer environment through small talk is to show enthusiasm for what the other person talks about. People like the feeling of being listened to, it makes them feel accepted and confident. If a man starts talking to you about his love of fishing, it is in your best interest to show enthusiasm about this topic, even if you don't like fishing at all. Get excited about what he is saying and ask him to tell you more about it. Ask questions, look engaged. When you do this, you may not be having a deep and meaningful conversation, but important bonding and human connection is happening underneath the surface. By simply listening and engaging with him on his fishing stories, you are telling him:

1. If it interests you, it interests me
2. I am a safe and fun person that you can talk to about anything
3. When you're around me, you will feel accepted and confident
4. I respect you and your interests

Many women can get this part wrong on the first date because they want to get to the good stuff. Remember Natalie? She was way too eager to pry sensitive information out of her date that she came across as aggressive and socially awkward. You don't want to be like Natalie, so you'll need to brush up on your small talk skills.

Something you may have noticed here is that the biggest part of being good at small talk is not really talking at all. It's about listening and showing the other person that you are interested in what *they* have to say. This is essential for building human connection because people love to talk about themselves and their interests. If you allow a man to talk about himself, you are going to make him feel funny, confident and entertaining, and he's going to love you for it.

Now let's not be ridiculous. I am not saying that you have to just let him yammer away the whole night and you never get to have a chance to talk. If he is a polite man with good social skills, he is going to ask you questions and listen to your stories as well. What needs to be remembered here is that when you're on date number one million and you have to tell *another guy* about what you do for fun *again,* it's not the topic of conversation that really matters, it's creating the safe environment so you can move on to more meaningful and engaging topics.

HAVING SELF-WORTH

The final dating emotion that I am going to talk about in this chapter is that of self-worth. Many successful women are blessed with having a sense of purpose. They are good at their job, they help their friends, they do volunteer work, etc. They have gone out of their way to feel like they are a value to others and contributing to society. The downfall of this is sometimes these women think that because of all that, they don't really deserve a loving partner. They feel like they have devoted their lives to other things and that maybe a romantic relationship just isn't for them.

A lot of times this also comes from the baggage of past relationships that were unhealthy. These wounds don't fully heal so in the back of your mind, you're thinking to yourself, maybe I'm just not cut out of this part of life. Maybe I've been blessed with so many other things that I'm not really deserving of a good relationship on top of everything else.

The first step that you can do to overcome this is to start believing that you are worthy of love. Show others love and kindness but know when to draw the line so that you're not getting taken advantage of. I came across an excellent quote one day that said, "you teach others how to treat you." If you are always really nice and never stand up for yourself, you're opening the doors for people who might abuse you. You have to be kind and loving to others but only if they deserve it. Especially in romantic relationships, you need to give as much as you receive. It should never be a one-way street.

On the flip side, giving people the benefit of the doubt goes a long way. When people make mistakes or show a moment of selfishness, it's not because they are trying to get you or intentionally hurt you. I have heard so many of my clients ask me "why would he do that?" and a lot of the time the answer is "because he was thinking of himself". You might have noticed that these last two paragraphs kind of contradict each other. One is saying stand up for yourself, the other is saying give him the benefit of the doubt. So, what are you supposed to do?

The best way to navigate this is the three chances rule. The first time he does something, let it go without talking to him about it. This will let you see if it was just a one-off thing. This will also stop you from having the never-ending "we need to talk" sessions after every little mishap. The second time he does something, have a talk with him about it. Tell him how it made you feel and come to an agreement. If he does it again, have one last talk with him. This time tell him the severity of the issue and how it makes you feel. If he continues to do it after this, decide if it's a deal-breaker if he never changes his ways. If it is, let him go.

The other side of "self-worth" is you need to balance inner self-confidence and vulnerability. We've been covering a lot in this chapter about confidence and personal revelation and now it's time to put the two together. When you have inner self-confidence and you are able to be open and welcome others, rejection hurts a lot less. Rejection should just sting a little and then you move on. The good news is that the more you stand up for yourself and open yourself up to others, the more likely you are to find a man who is willing to do the same. People mirror each other.

Have you ever noticed that when you raise your voice in a conversation, the other person immediately starts talking louder? People mirror each other so the more open and sharing you are, the more open and sharing others will be with you. Just remember that you don't need to reveal everything right away. Put yourself out there but reveal your vulnerability step by step. Slowly take the wall down when the right person comes along. There's nothing wrong with getting your feet wet first and testing the waters before you dive in – in fact, it's probably very smart.

CHAPTER SIX

How To Play The Dating Game

ALRIGHT, ENOUGH IS ENOUGH WITH THE mindset stuff. Let's get into the nitty-gritty! In this chapter, we'll be talking about the dating game and how you can play this game to your advantage. There are unwritten rules in dating. You probably know some of them, even many of them, but not all of them.

This chapter is all about actionable steps. You have already learned that you should work on your self-confidence, your small talk skills, your ability to be vulnerable, etc. This chapter will tell you when, where and how much of those skills should be used. Let's take a look.

LET HIM TAKE (MOST OF) THE LEAD

This is one thing you have to understand when dating men. Men don't need your help when it comes to locking down the woman of their dreams. When they are in love, they will act like it; and you can thank society for that one. Men have learned that if they don't make the first move, they might get left high and dry. They know it's their role in society to be the one to make the decisions. In other words, he *knows* it's his job to ask you out and text you because if he doesn't do those things, *you* might not do them. If he doesn't say "hey, let's go to the movies" then he knows there's a big chance that he won't be going to the movies with you.

Remember the old days? When a gentleman opened the door for a woman, and pulled the chair out for her so she could sit down? Although that kind of chivalry might be dead in the water, men have been conditioned for generations to be make an impression and be respectful if they want to get the attention of a high-quality woman. Let's take an example out from my real life. I was playing matchmaker with two friends of mine. I had set up a male friend and a female friend and they were really hitting it off. The best part about this for me was that I could hear both sides of the story and study exactly what was going on. The couple had been on a few dates and my female friend, let's call her Elizabeth, had been feeling excited about her new man, let's call him Anthony, but she wasn't quite ready to take things to the next level.

Anthony was excited about Elizabeth as well but wanted to tread the waters carefully since they had a lot of mutual friends and he didn't want to come across as too eager. Elizabeth then told me that Anthony was asking her over to his house. Her being a woman, automatically assumed that he was doing this in order to get the sexual relationship started. He was probably going to make a sexual move and she really wasn't ready to go in that direction, so she hesitated to go to his house.

Lucky me, I get to hear both sides of the story, so I casually asked him how things were going. He said to me that he was dying to get Elizabeth over to his house because he really wanted to show her that he knows how to cook. He really wanted to impress her with his cooking skills. See? When a man is excited and interested in you, he will go out of his way to treat you like a lady and impress you. Does he want to get you into bed? Sure, but if he really likes you, he wants to respect your wishes and act like a gentleman.

So, what do you do in an early relationship that is just starting to take off to help move things to the next step? Nothing! That's right, just let him do most of the work. Let him ask you out. Let him initiate text conversations or phone calls. Let him follow up with you after the date and say how much fun he had. He won't take the lead forever, just until he's your boyfriend.

DON'T LISTEN TO YOUR ANXIETY

Some people have a much easier time letting the man lead than others. People with an anxious attachment style or people who are type A and like to plan things can struggle with taking a back seat. If this is you, I assure you, your overthinking anxious behavior is not going to help you land that guy.

Dating is all about setting a certain standard with the person that you are with. I have a client who got out of a very bad relationship. In this relationship, she told me how she dated a man for seven years who would constantly call her names and swear to her. If she didn't make him dinner that night, he would ask her why she's "being so bitchy." Arguments with him were always about him being "fucking pissed" and would involve a lot of yelling and raising of voices.

Now I am not for one second saying that any of this man's behavior is the fault of my client. However, at the beginning when he first showed signs of yelling or swearing, she should have told him to either cut that out or she's going to leave, or she should have just left. When you put up and accept bad behavior, it's not your fault that the behavior is happening, but it's your fault that you are deciding to stay in the relationship despite it. I know it's not always easy to get out if you've been together for years and your lives are intertwined. This is why you absolutely must be on the lookout when you're just dating.

When you're dating, men can show bad behavior that you should not put up with. If he hasn't texted you for a week, you might feel this undeniable need to text him to see what's going on. Don't listen to this urge. This is your anxiety talking. It is your fear of being left behind and it will not help you to constantly satisfy those urges by texting or checking in with the other person. You need to find a better outlet for your energy.

THE RULES OF TEXTING

Texting is a fairly new thing when it comes to the history of dating. Texting is much like birth control in the sense that humans were doing something one way for centuries and then BAM! Something else showed up that completely changed the game. Now even if you don't really enjoy texting or don't think it has enough of a personal touch, it's something you're going to need to understand if you want to date past the year 2007.

First things first, it's ok to text him first. There's nothing wrong with being the one to initiate conversation. I have been a matchmaker and coach to many men and let me tell you something, they *love* it when a woman shows she is interested. It makes it a little easier for them to open up, you know? If he has to be the one to start the conversations all the time, he's going to question whether or not you're even into this. That's not the way you want to make the man you like feel. You want to be doing things to boost his confidence not tear it down.

You're probably thinking "Hey, I thought you said to let him take the lead?" It's true I did say that, but if you flip back a couple of pages to the heading of that section, you'll see I said *Let Him Take MOST of the Lead*. See dating, is a bit of a game. You both have to do a little "yeah, I'm interested, whoops not THAT interested, ok yeah I'm interested." It's a bit of a back and forth of revealing how much you like each other without being *too* revealing. Many women (and men) are tired of this dating game so they want to fight it. They ask me, "why do we have to play these games, why can't we just be honest with each other?" The answer is, chemistry! You might not like playing the game, but if it wasn't there, the romance would not be any fun at all. Think about it. The texts would look something like this. He's the first text, you are the second and it alternates back and forth.

"Hey, your profile is actually pretty good and I think you're hot, do you like my profile?

"Yeah, it's not the worst I've seen, I'm interested in feeling this out."

"Cool, do you want to meet for drinks or should we just pretend we're interested in this conversation for a bit?"

"I'd like to pretend for a bit. I've been on a lot of dates and this is kind of the way I filter if it's going to be worth my time."

"Yeah no worries, I get it. I like to play soccer, go hiking and I'm a software developer. Are any of those things deal breakers?"

"Nah, you're good so far. I'm a nurse, I like painting/art and yeah I also like hiking."

"Sweet! Something in common. Where do you hike? Should we make that our first date?"

"No, that's a little creepy, can we just do the drinks?"

"Yeah, let's do drinks."

"Great, here's my number, it's a date."

Now I know you're thinking, "OMG" if the world were like this it would be *so much easier* to date! Yeah, you're not wrong. It would definitely be *easier,* but it would also be boring and not very romantic. There's no "spark", build up or teasing with conversations like this. There's also a misalignment of goals because women and men are looking for different things at the beginning of a relationship.

Men want to get you into bed, so his version of not "playing the game" and skipping the teasing is just straight up asking you "so, do you want to bump uglies?" That's not something that is very romantic or appealing to you. On your side, you're likely looking to see if he's interested in an actual relationship and if he meets your standards, your version of skipping the dating game would be asking him: "hey are you emotionally and financially stable enough to commit to me long-term and provide for our future family?" That's not appealing to him at all.

So, there you have it. The dating "game" and the back and forth teasing and anticipation are there because men and women have different goals when it comes to dating and they must meet in the middle.

So yes, you can take the lead sometimes and send a text to start a conversation. The issue lies in the frequency of the initial text. This means how often *you* text first without letting *him* text first. You want to text him first once in a while to show that you're interested, but you don't want to text too often because that can show that you're desperate or too eager – not attractive qualities. The magic number is to keep the ratio roughly 2:1. If he has initiated the last two conversations, it's your turn to start a conversation.

That being said, don't get too caught up in the numbers. If you're constantly counting conversations and texts, you're surely overthinking it. The only reason I make these numbers specific is so that you have a general idea of what is expected. I do this so that a woman who thinks it's ok to text a man five times throughout the day when he barely responds back will know that she is overdoing it. If you find that you're the one always texting first, you should definitely pull back the reigns a bit and let him take more of the lead.

Next, we should talk about emojis. I came across an article saying that people over the age of 16 shouldn't use emojis. This is crazy! Emojis play a very important role in texting conversations. They are not childish or immature if used in the right way. Text-based conversations are extremely difficult to portray emotion and intonation. A reader can view a text as aggressive when really it was just a sarcastic and harmless comment. So how do we increase the chances that our messages are getting across in the right tone? Emojis! I can't imagine having a cheeky or sarcastic conversation without the use of a wink face or sticking out tongue to say "I'm only joking." So keep using them, but as always – don't go overboard.

Next, you have to text according to his effort. If you haven't heard from a guy in weeks and he texts you "hey, sup?" Don't respond back with an overly detailed re-cap of what your life has been like for the weeks where he ghosted you. Reply to a no-effort text like that with the same amount of effort. Something like "I'm good, you?" will suffice. Remember that letting the man take the lead is still valid here. If he's been ignoring you or flaky, don't give him the time and attention that he's asking for until he deserves it.

Men have been taught by society since the beginning of dating that if they don't make the effort to reach out to the woman, they may not get a date. If he is interested in you, he will 100% reach out. So, what does this mean for you?

No texting 'hey, haven't heard from you in a while"

No Texting "hey, I miss you"

Don't send follow up texts if you don't hear back.
It's also good to pay attention to the time of day when he's texting you. Does he text you late at night when he's bored or looking for a booty call? Or does he text you during the day, genuinely asking how your day is going? Are the texts strictly texts or does he move the

interactions forward by asking you out or asking for a phone call? You don't want a pen pal. You want texting to be a way to lead up to the next date. Too much texting without a date planned is not a good sign. All of these things are ways for you to see how much effort he's putting forward. Your level of effort should always match his.

The last thing we need to cover about texting and communication with your new man is to always stay honest and genuine. Don't try to manipulate him or "test" him by sending certain texts. For example, let's' say you ignore one of his texts just to see if he'll text you after you've ignored him. If he does text you, you think "Yes! He *does* like me". This is unhealthy manipulation and you know who's going to get hurt by doing this? You! That's right, manipulation and unhealthy game playing will backfire on your confidence and self-esteem so it's best not to get involved with it. Any texts that might be passive-aggressive, asking for attention or manipulative should be kept out. You want to start off with a healthy relationship, not an unhealthy one!

EFFORT WORTHINESS

One important thing I want to mention while we're on the topic of the dating game is effort worthiness. Effort worthiness is the amount of effort you deserve from someone. It is earned over time so when you've just matched someone on a dating app or you're just messaging back and forth, you have not earned any effort worthiness so you shouldn't really expect much. Let's look at a real-life example.

My boyfriend and I have been dating for years and we live together so our lives are very intertwined. If I asked him to take the day off work because I'm deathly ill and need him to take care of me all day, depending on the circumstances, he might actually do this. That is a huge favor to ask from someone, but since I have earned a lot of effort worthiness, it is something I can ask of him and something that he would consider doing. He would be willing to put in that amount of effort because I am that worthy of it. But there was a time when my effort worthiness was nowhere near this high. When we first started talking to each other, he was simply another one of my matches on Tinder.

On Tinder, I had a list of matches and some of them I liked better than others. The profile of the man who is currently my boyfriend and the love of my life had a profile that I liked more than others yet he wasn't messaging me. Back then I had not earned any "effort worthiness" from him so I shouldn't even expect him to send me a little message. I was just a photo on a screen, I didn't mean anything to him. Sure, it's nice when the guy messages first, but this is by no means a requirement and I shouldn't make it a requirement for no reason. Instead of staying at zero effort worthiness, I decided to shoot him a message. Now I wasn't just a photo on a screen, I was a photo and a message. After we started chatting, I let him take the lead. He had to be the one to ask me out on a date and multiple dates after that.

The rest is history and we have been happily dating ever since, but the point I'm trying to make is when you're just a photo on a screen, you don't mean to anything to him. If you want to see if the two of you will be a good fit, message him first, chat back and forth and you could even ask him out on the first date. The more he gets to know you, the more effort worthiness you are building up and the more you can expect from him. If you set up and plan the first date, then at least the date is planned and you can see if the two of you actually like each other.

All of that being said, it all ends after the first date. After you've met, you should pull back and let him take the lead. I don't want you to make all the moves, simply two moves: the first message, and asking him out on the first date, if he doesn't do it after enough messaging. The effort you expect from a man at the beginning, when you don't even know each other, should be minimal.

As mentioned, this "effort worthiness" strategy should only be used up until you have had your first date. Then you must adopt the "Thank you, Next" strategy.

THE "THANK YOU, NEXT" STRATEGY

We can all learn a little something from Ariana Grande. This strategy is something that will keep you from feeling heartbroken, stop you from wasting time and find you a relationship with someone that is 100% and totally into you. The strategy is simple on paper but hard to practice. It can be summed up as follows: *If a man wants to be your boyfriend, he will act like your boyfriend.*

It seems quite simple, doesn't it? Yet we often find ourselves in a situation where we're saying things like:

"He hasn't called or texted in a couple of weeks"

"Everything was going great and now he's saying he wants to keep things casual"

"We've been dating for 3 months but he still doesn't call me his girlfriend."

All of these are examples of women who haven't perfected the "thank you, next" strategy. When a man is interested, he doesn't just ignore you or call it casual. He wants to hang out with you, have sex with you and lock you down so that other men won't take you away. Unless we're talking about polyamorous or open relationships, most men who are interested in you for the long-term do NOT want you sleeping with other guys! Think about it. A man finds a sexy, smart and amazing woman that he is falling head over heels for. If he is considering a relationship with her, he doesn't want her sleeping with other men behind his back. He's going to make things official pretty quick to let her know that he wants her.

Let's look at it from another angle, the angle of falling in love. Remember how you felt the last time you were falling for someone? You were thinking about him all the time, you wanted to text him, you wanted to hang out with him. You were attracted to him and wanted to be in his presence at nearly every moment.

Ready for the shocking newsflash?

Men who are in love feel the exact same way! When a man is falling for an amazing woman, he *wants* to spend time with her. Men don't need a lot of "thinking time" when it comes to dating. If he seems hesitant or distant, then he's not "figuring things out" to see if he wants to move forward, he is just straight up not that interested. Let's use a little science to help take this point home. A study published on Askmen.com confirmed that men are more impulsive than women. When they feel a spark, they go all in, no need to think about it.

"You've heard it before, but for men, when something is special about a woman, they'll jump on it. That's why you'll hear many people say that "a man's light was on" when he decided to get married: once [a man makes] a decision about a person or a time of [his] life that [he's] ready for, [he's] all in. Women are a little more analytical about everything and will often think through the relationship's longevity more thoroughly than [men] will. "By nature, men can act more impulsively when they feel something, where women need to be more certain and cautious," Martinez says. "Men are okay with jumping in and trying a new relationship when they feel the right connection instead of being cautious and waiting until they know for sure like a woman might do." (Tigar, 2019)

When I read this study and others saying similar things, it was like a light bulb went off in my head. Not only did this make a lot of sense, it just made dating a hell of a lot easier! Dating used to be so complicated. When you're sitting at home wondering if he's going to text you or wondering what happened to him, the answer to "what should I do?" becomes so simple:

"**Thank you** for the fun time, onto the **next** one."

This mentality is not only empowering, but it also calms the overthinking racing brain. Men are not subtle. They do not like to hint. If they are interested, you will know. It will be glaringly obvious.

WHAT HAPPENED? HE JUST...GHOSTED ME.

The next thing we are going to talk about is the "ghost". This happens to pretty much everyone when they are out there on the dating scene. You're having a great time with a guy you just met. He asks you out on dates, he texts you, you're having great sex and then suddenly, you don't hear from him again. Now if we're following the "thank you, next" strategy, you'll know that you shouldn't chase him or try to force anything because he clearly wasn't interested. Yet, you can't help but wonder... *what happened?* Here is where science is going to come to the rescue again. See men and women experience attraction a little differently than each other and understanding this difference is going to help explain why this happens.

See, men are physical attraction first, personality second. Women are personality and emotional bonding first, physical attraction second.

So when you're on a first date with a guy, you've seen his basic appearance and you've decided "this will do" and from then on, you're analyzing and critiquing every aspect of his personality. If he talks too long about himself, that's a turnoff. If he doesn't pay for dinner, that's a turnoff. If he mentions he is into hunting, that's either a turnoff or a turn on but either way, you're trying to get a sense of his entire personality based on one interest, hobby or comment. In a nutshell, once you have decided that his physical appearance is good enough, you will spend the rest of the time figuring out if his personality lives up to your standards and if he is going to make a good long-term partner. I'm sorry to be the one to tell you this but... men don't do it this way.

Instead, he is taking way more time to analyze how "hot" you are and how much he is attracted to you physically. This means he is looking at your smile, your body movements, your overall appearance and mannerisms to see if you have physical chemistry. In other words, if he is very physically attracted to you, that comes first and your personality comes second. This can be proven easily if you have ever had any male friends. How many of your male friends have started seeing a totally bat-shit crazy woman just because she was really hot? This happens all the time! Let's take a look at this study from Medicis Aesthetics to make things a little clearer:

*"In a study commissioned by **Medicis Aesthetics**, 1,000 men and women were polled on many relationship questions — from marriage and divorce to physical attraction. What they found was that while looks mattered to both sexes, for men especially, how their potential partner looked was much more important — and a bigger indicator of overall*

attraction. "Men are initially attracted to women based on a **physical connection** and then grow to love the person," Martinez says. "They do not think someone is nice and then have the attraction grow." (Tigar, 2019)

This explains why men are so much more likely to ghost you and disappear after seemingly having a lot of fun. It's because if they find you physically attractive, they are going to have a lot of fun hanging out with you and having sex with you because that is all they are prioritizing at the moment. Then eventually, they will start to decide if your personality is something that fits with them for the long-term. If they decide the answer to this is "no" they will move onto someone else. This might sound harsh but really, it's only fair. You have all your standards and checkboxes for things you want in a man. You want to make sure he has a good job, is family-oriented, is intelligent, etc. He has every right to have his checklist as well. The problem here is that both of you are running through the checklists at different times.

You're running through the checklist on the first date and every date after that. If you are interested in seeing him for date number two, this means he didn't do anything to rule him out of "long-term" potential, yet if he wants to see *you* for date number two, this is just because he thinks you're hot. He hasn't even begun to decide if you have long-term potential yet. He'll decide this later, *once you've already started falling for him.* If he decides that he doesn't think you're long-term potential, you'll end up ghosted or broken up with even though "things were going so well."

So there you have it! Men just go through the "long-term partner" checklist a little later than women. Now that you know this, it's even more important to analyze the way a man is treating you in the beginning stages. Does he just want to take you out for late-night drinks and then back to his place? Or does he want to spend the whole day at the beach talking and getting to know you? If the dates he chooses are about getting to know your personality and he is willing to spend time talking to you instead of just having sex, you'll see that he is interested in more than just a physical relationship.

YOUR FIRST DATE VIBE IS SO IMPORTANT

Earlier in this book, you learned that creating a "safe environment" through small talk is a way to help the other person open up. This is part of what I call the "first date vibe". You see, it is impossible to know someone's entire personality on the first date so the first date is not really about your individual personalities, it's about the vibe. It's about energy.

You are trying to see if he makes you feel safe, secure and listened to. He is trying to see if you are going to be fun in the bedroom. If you are interested in a man and want to help make sure he is interested in you, it's best to make your first date vibe "light-hearted and fun." This tells him, you're easy-going and non-judgemental. There is nothing more attractive to a man than a woman who just wants to have fun and doesn't want to get serious right away because as we learned before, all he cares about right now is the "fun" part, he's not thinking about the long-term potential stuff just yet.

Now don't get me wrong, I don't want you to just jump into bed with him. I just don't want you to come across as uptight or too serious. Asking him questions about marriage, kids or other long-term topics make it seem to him that you are way too eager to settle down.

Remember, he is just trying to figure out if you're "hot" and does not want to think about settling down just yet so keeping your "first date vibe" fun is key.

TURN UP THE FEMININE ENERGY

I'm throwing this one in because I struggled with this a lot when I was younger. I considered myself a strong woman. I had a good career. I was financially independent, had a strong social circle, hobbies and was very self-confident. I didn't really need a man and I definitely wasn't desperate, but I wanted someone by my side. I guess I was missing a bit of a romantic connection in my life.

Now I'm a feminist just like you, I believe in equality for women in all aspects of life. You are strong and driven and you know this because you have reached high achievements. You are very successful and you're proud of it, but when you're dating, you're in the most primal of situations. It is best to tap into your feminine energy and use that on dates – because it's more attractive to men. Now, you don't want to be faking your personality or anything like that, but the good news is you don't have to. If you are a woman, you have both feminine and masculine qualities. It's in your best interest to bring those feminine qualities to the forefront. Feminine energy is generally more caring and compassionate, otherwise known as "responsiveness". Researchers from the Interdisciplinary Center (IDC) Herzliya, the University of Rochester, and the University of Illinois at Urbana-Champaign held studies to see how men were attracted to responsive women versus un-responsive women. Here is what they found:

"Participants in the second study were asked to interact with a responsive or non-responsive individual of the opposite sex, and view that individual's photo (the same photo was given to each participant). They were then asked to interact online with this individual and discuss details on a current problem in their life. The responsiveness of the virtual individual was manipulated, for example, "You must have gone through a very difficult time" as a responsive reply, versus "Doesn't sound so bad to me" as a non-responsive reply."

"Men who interacted with a responsive female individual perceived her as more feminine and as more sexually attractive than did men in the unresponsive condition." (Science Daily, 2014)

I used to work a corporate job surrounded by men, and one thing that you quickly learn in this kind of professional environment is not to be very emotional. If you're seen crying or getting stressed out, it could make you look really bad in these hostile and male-dominated workforces. If you have one of these jobs, you might have taught yourself to bury emotions. If you take one thing away from this book, it should be that your emotions and *giving* nature as a woman are attractive to men. They want to see that feminine side of you that is friendly and nurturing. In fact, having dealt with many male clients as a matchmaker, I find that one of the most common traits they want to see in their partner is an element of "playfulness". I've even heard some men describe it as "almost childlike." Although a little creepy and off-putting at first, you can kind of picture what they mean. They want the silliness, innocence, and playfulness that comes with feminine energy. Your stoic and professional personality has made you very successful at work, but could be hurting your dating life.

Another aspect that comes with feminine energy is the idea of "needing a man". Now I know the title of this book and I'm not about to throw a curveball here, but part of feminine energy is making your man feel like he is needed. The truth is, as a single woman, you don't need a man and you can live a perfectly happy and healthy life without one. Yet, if you find a man that you really love, and you *want* to include him in your life – he will want to feel like he is needed. Like he is integrated into your life in a way that makes it very difficult for you to let him go. You would appreciate the same treatment from him. If you have given up years of your life to settle down with a man, you wouldn't want him to say that he doesn't need you around. Once you decide to (willingly) let a man into your life, it's in your best interest to let him know that you appreciate him being part of your life. At the beginning stages of dating, this can be saying things like:

"You are so fun to be around after a boring day at work."

"You always take me to the coolest restaurants."

"I feel so comfortable around you."

Then once you have a more established relationship you can start giving deeper and more revealing compliments like "I am so happy that we're together" or "I don't know what I'd do without you." These compliments are not desperate or needy, they tell your man that the two of you have a bond and that you're happy to have that bond with him. Compliments like this strengthen your emotional bond and make your relationship happy and healthier.

WHEN TO HAVE SEX

Ah, the big question! This was what you came here for wasn't it? Well not so fast my friend, because this is one of the most nuanced and complicated aspects of dating. If you've read my blog, you know that I have a "magic number" that I tell my readers as well as my coaching clients, but this magic number isn't to be used "willy nilly". This number comes with a lot of responsibility and an overall understanding of the role sex plays in the early stages of a relationship. Take a deep breath, let's dive into this.

My first long-term relationship was fun, lasted three years and ended when I discovered he was cheating on me. I believe we dated for about a whole year and we were definitely boyfriend and girlfriend before we had sex. My second relationship ended after four years and we waited about four weeks before we had sex. In my third long-term relationship, the one that is currently going strong, we waited for about *three dates* before we had sex. Are you seeing a pattern here? Well, I hope not, because there isn't one. Let me just burn this into your head right now:

There is no perfect or set amount of dates you should wait before having sex with a new man.

Phew! Now that we have that out of the way, there are things that we need to take into consideration so that we can make healthy decisions about this. The first thing is you have to understand your attachment style and how attached you get to men that you've had sex with. I have a female client that is very good at having no strings attached sex. She can just go out, meet a man, have sex and not have any emotional feelings tied to the act. On the flip side, I know that I am personally not like this. I was in a friends with benefits relationship with someone that I was not attracted to, never wanted to date, didn't really like his personality and we didn't get along that well and yet, I still found myself feeling emotionally attached only because we were doing the dirty. If you're like me, it's going to be better to wait longer before you have sex. If you're like my client, you won't have to wait as long. I didn't wait long enough when I started dating my current boyfriend. Had he not been interested in me after that third date, I would have been devastated. I was really risking my emotions and mental well-being when I had sex with him so early. I got lucky.

The timing of sex that is right for you is something only you can determine because everyone's relationship with sex is different. Some people have a very high libido and they enjoy a physical release when they have sex. Other people have lower libido and are more likely to tie sex with a bonding act rather than needing that physical simulation. It's in your best interest to sit down and think long and hard about where you might land on this spectrum and act accordingly.

Now I'm going to discuss something that a lot of dating coaches avoid talking about. The truth is, if you have been single and do not like hooking up with random men on a one night stand, you've probably gone a couple of months (or more) without having sex. This means that the second you find someone who is attractive, funny and you're really interested in, you're going to want to jump his bones like it's your last day on earth. Seriously, your sex hormones are going to be driving you crazy. It is for THIS reason that I like to say to my clients, please for the love of God wait for at least five dates before you have sex.

I find that this number is a very realistic minimum number to hit. If I told you to wait until you're married, that probably wouldn't happen. If I told you to wait until you're exclusive, again, probably a little too long for your raging sex hormones. Yet, five dates is reasonable, manageable and something we can pretty much all hit if we try. If you wait longer, that's even better because it allows you to test the waters and see if you're interested in this man for the long-term. It also gives you a better filter. See, a man who is interested in you as a long-term, marriage potential partner is going to *want* to have sex with you but he will also respect your wishes if you want take things slow. A man that is just in it for the wham bam, thank you ma'am is going to be less inclined to wine and dine you for more than a couple dates without getting laid.

Now I wish that I could just end this section on sex right here because that would make things very neat and tidy. You learned that you have to wait for at least five dates but the longer the better so that you can filter out the players who just want to have sex. This is good advice but the truth is, those "player" guys who just want to have a one night stand are pretty easy to spot. We can pretty much see what a man's intentions are after a dick pic or suggestive text or comment – it's really not that difficult. The tricky part comes with the "nice guy". The man that wants to take you for dates wants to hang out with you, wants to have sex but then just never makes the next move to make the two of you official. Months start going by and you're still not sure if you're boyfriend and girlfriend. The way we avoid this kind of dead-end casual relationship is directly related to sex.

When you start having sex with a new man, your relationship is supposed to be getting stronger. This means that not only are you releasing your feel-good sexual hormones, both of you should also be feeling the "love dovey" hormones. The ones that make you feel bonded and tied to the person emotionally. If you are in a casual relationship with a man that has no intention of making you his girlfriend, he won't be feeling those "love" hormones. He's just in it for the sex.

The first way you can filter out if he's just in it for the sex is by paying attention to how he wants to spend time with you. Does he want to go out with you on long, all-day dates or does he just want some quick drinks after work and then head to his place after? Men who are in love will want to take you out on activities and have longer dates that are not booty calls.

Does he sleepover after he has sex? This one is big. He doesn't have to sleep over every time, sometimes he really might have to wake up early or have to get back to his place but if you've been seeing each other for more than a month and there haven't been any sleepovers, this is a red flag.

Another thing you have to look out for is his willingness to introduce you to other aspects of his life. Does he want you to meet his friends? His family? If you invite him out to meet your friends, does he want to go along? If he wants to be part of your life outside the bedroom, this is a good sign, if he doesn't – run! Those are signs that you should be looking out for when you're entering a new relationship, but there is one hard and fast actionable task that you can adopt in your dating life so you're never stuck in a relationship limbo ever again. That is the "exclusivity" talk.

When a man and a woman start having sex in a casual manner, they don't necessarily need to be exclusive to one another. They can still be seeing and sleeping with other people and still have this casual relationship. Most of the time, when two people are falling in love and really like each other, they will start having sex and hanging out but the "exclusivity" talk doesn't come up until both of them are ready to make more of a commitment. So here's the hard and fast rule:

There is no "exclusive" without being boyfriend and girlfriend.

There you go! You've done it. This means that if he wants the privilege of having you not sleep or see any other men, he will need to start calling you his girlfriend. So if he brings up the idea that he is not seeing any other women and he doesn't want you to see other men, you can tell him that sounds like a good plan so that means you are now boyfriend and girlfriend. If he's not comfortable with that, just tell him that you would like to be boyfriend and girlfriend before making things exclusive.

This is a huge bargaining chip and a super easy way to see if he's interested in you for the long-term. If he is really interested in you and is falling for you, he won't like the idea that you might be seeing other men. To top off this rule, don't remain in a casual non-exclusive relationship for more than two months. If you follow these rules, you will be able to use sex in a healthy way and you'll never be caught in a never-ending casual scenario.

MAKE HIM FEEL GOOD

Remember at the very beginning of this book how I said that modern women don't need a relationship, they just want one? Well, men are in the same boat. They don't need to marry you to have sex, they don't need to take on all the household bills because society told them to and they don't need to put up with a bad relationship for any kind of social approval or status. So why does he need a relationship? Because hopefully, it makes him feel good – and that's where you come in.

When a man is dating a new woman, he wants her to think he's the sexiest, funniest, most masculine guy around. He wants to impress her but he also, wants her to *be impressed*. When you are in the beginning stages of a relationship, it does you no good to think about when he's going to text you next or what it meant when he said "this" or "that". Instead, just focus on making him feel good and seeing if he does the same in return. No, I do not mean sexually. I mean emotionally. I'm not saying you should fake anything, but just make an effort to show him how fun and loving you are, trust me, he'll repay you in more ways than one.

In this chapter, you learned how to play the dating game. You learned that there is a little bit of healthy game playing involved in dating because it sparks anticipation and chemistry. You're just about set and ready to conquer the dating game, but there's one last step. You need to know how to pick a man who is worth your time.

CHAPTER SEVEN

How To Find The One Who Is Worth Your Time

MY BROTHER IN LAW WAS SPENDING THE afternoon fishing on a dock. He sat there patiently waiting for that bite to hit when suddenly it did. He felt the tug on his line and excitedly started winding up the rod. I had never seen someone catch a fish before, so I was intrigued and watching closely. Once he had the rod wound up, he grabbed the fish in his hand, gave it a long stare, pulled the hook out of its mouth and tossed it back in the water.

"What? Why did you throw him back in?" I asked.

"Meh, he's too small, I'm waiting for the big one." He replied.

My brother in law is an expert fisherman. He knows that if he waits around, the better fish will come along, and you will be like this in dating. Always waiting for the big one and never settling for the little bottom feeder just because he's in your hand. Let's take a look at exactly how we can make that happen. First, you need to understand that as a woman, you have been biologically wired to think of the other person first – and this can really hurt your chances of finding a great guy and not settling for less.

WOMEN ARE MORE SELFLESS THAN MEN

Yes, it is true, women are naturally more giving and selfless than men. The studies prove it!

"Conventional wisdom, and much research suggests women tend to be more other-oriented than men. Two very different new studies confirm this vexing gender imbalance—one by looking at brain activity, the other by examining the behavior of new parents.

The first finds the neural reward system of women is triggered by generosity, while that of men is more stimulated by self-centeredness. The second reports that, according to a survey of dual-earner households, new fathers manage to carve out far more leisure time for themselves than do new mothers." (Jacobs, 2017)

This reveals a lot about the different ways men and women approach life. See, women are more likely to want to please others, they are willing to give up their personal wants and needs. Men are more likely to act on their own emotions. They don't do something if they don't want to. They don't go out of their way for someone if it's not going to benefit them. Remember, I am speaking in very broad, general terms that are based on statistics. I'm not saying all men are selfish, just that they are likely to listen to their own needs first. So what ends happening to women that put others before themselves? They build up resentment. See, we women put others before ourselves because it's wired in our biology but that doesn't mean we always *want* to do this. We feel pressure or we feel like we should, but too much giving makes us bitter, angry and stressed because we have too much on our plate, too little time and we feel like we are taking care of everything and everyone.

This plays a major role in our relationships as well. We often adopt the role of the "mother" taking care of our significant other or giving them too much benefit of the doubt. Instead, we need to find someone that complements us and helps us where we need support as well. It is for this reason that you must find a partner that you are compatible with. One way to help determine this is by looking at the big five personality traits.

THE BIG FIVE PERSONALITY TRAITS

Although any kind of system or set of rules that lump humans into labels or stereotypes should be taken with a grain of salt, the truth is there are many personality traits that can be grouped into overall, larger categories. Understanding these categories can help us predict the kind of person we are getting involved with, so this a great way to look at a potential romantic partner and their ability to be compatible with your personality.

One set of categories is called the "Big Five Personality Traits". These traits are genetic traits that you were born with and although it's not impossible, they are very difficult to change once you become an adult. This is because there are two aspects to every human's personality. Those that were given to us by *nature* and those that were given to us by *nurture*. These big five personality traits are what nature intended for us and they have a very crucial role in picking a romantic partner that is going to turn into a successful relationship. Here are how the big five personality traits can predict your relationship success.

First and foremost, it is important to understand each trait and what they mean. All five traits can easily be remembered with the acronym OCEAN, which stands for Openness, Conscientiousness, Extroversion, Agreeableness, and Neuroticism. Each of these traits also has a polar opposite and your dominant traits will land somewhere along a spectrum. Here I have placed a chart that shows each trait on the appropriate spectrum. You will naturally land somewhere on this spectrum.

BIG 5 PERSONALITY TRAITS

Low Score		High Score
Traditional, likes routine	Openness To Experience	Impulsive, independent
Impulsive, careless	Conscientiousness	Organized, dependable
Quiet, reserved	Extroversion	Social, outgoing
Critical, suspicious	Agreeableness	Helpful, empathetic
Calm, even tempered	Neuroticism	Prone to negative emotions

YOU ARE NOT ONE TRAIT OR THE OTHER

Before I dive into the five traits in detail, it is important to note that these traits represent the extremes. You cannot say you are "open to experience" and not "traditional" because that simply isn't true. You have a little bit of both sides of the spectrum in your personality, but you will lean towards one more than the other. No one will ever be 100% one trait. I also want to point out that these traits *can* be changed, but where you naturally land on the spectrum is going to determine the level of effort required to change. Let's look at extroversion vs introversion as an example.

Let's say that you took a test and the result was that you are 25% extroverted, meaning that you are an introvert because your score was less than 50%. Now let's say that you'd like to be the top salesman for an alarm company. This requires you to be more extroverted, so you start trying to actively change your personality to become more extroverted. You go to improv classes, public speaking classes and read books on improving your social skills. You are trying very hard to be more extroverted and thus, a better salesman. After all that education and practice, you may now score 60% on the extroversion spectrum. Compare that to someone who just naturally scored 75% and you'd still be more introverted than them despite all that work! So yes, you can change aspects of your personality but where you naturally land as a result of your genetics is going to be the most determining factor in how you behave. Now let's take this information and apply it to relationships.

The person you are seeing should have personality traits that compliment yours. Otherwise, it's going to be *very difficult* to get them to change. This is why so many people end up with an incompatible partner. A partner with whom they face so many relationship troubles despite discussions, deep personal talks and even relationship counseling. Have you ever been in one of those relationships where you're always having to "talk"? "We need to talk", "let's talk, there's something bothering me". These talks are exhausting! When you're in a relationship with someone that is compatible with you, these "talks" happen only once in a blue moon and you spend the rest of your time having fun!

Let's look at how these traits will play in a relationship. Let's use the introvert/extrovert example again. I personally score around 45% on the extroversion spectrum meaning that I am mostly introverted but still land somewhat close to the 50% mark. My ex-boyfriend probably would have scored around the 10% mark on the spectrum meaning that he never wanted to go out and hang out with my friends and had a very difficult time keeping friends of his own. We struggled a lot because I would want to go out or have friends come over and he was never into it. It made him very uncomfortable because he so much hated being social with people.

This resulted in a lot of frustration, discussions and me trying to fit a square peg into a round hole. In this case, the ball would be in my court and I would have to decide if I'm okay with being in a relationship where my boyfriend never goes out with me in public. There is no right or wrong answer, but I personally chose that I wasn't okay with this and thus we became incompatible.

Now I have a boyfriend who scores about 35% on the extroversion spectrum. This means he's slightly less extroverted than I am, but our compatibility is a lot more in line. What does this mean for me?

- No fighting about hanging out with my friends
- I never have to beg him to take me out on dates
- No trying to force him into situations that he doesn't want to be in
- He's not so extroverted that he's dragging me out to social events that I don't want to be a part of

Now that you see how important personality compatibility is for a successful relationship, I am going to go into each of these in detail. It will help you keep an eye out for what to look for when you're dating. You want to find a man with a personality that compliments yours.

OPENNESS

Scoring high on this trait means that you have a vivid imagination and are curious about the world. You are eager to partake in new experiences, learn new things and step out of your comfort zone. You are also less likely to simply take people's advice and are more willing to experience things on your own before you make a decision.

People who score low on this trait are more traditional and structured. They enjoy routine, do not like change and do not enjoy stepping out of their comfort zone.

IMPACT ON YOUR RELATIONSHIP

Someone scoring high in openness is going to be an adventure seeker and might have trouble settling down and living a routine life. They enjoy new experiences and have creative and vivid imaginations. If you score low on this trait, you want to be with someone who also scores low because you'll both be content with a more routine life. The white picket fence with a house in the suburbs is more likely to fit someone low on this trait. However, if you like adventure, traveling and trying new things, you might want to be with someone who also shares those values and also scores high here.

CONSCIENTIOUSNESS

Scoring high in conscientiousness means you are organized and have a strong work ethic. You enjoy setting goals, making a plan to reach those goals and sticking to the plan until the goal has been reached. These people tend to be more "Type A" personalities, the ones that like making to-do lists and creating spreadsheets. Scoring high in this trait also means that you don't like to procrastinate, and you adhere to a set schedule.

Scoring low on this trait means that you are impulsive. You don't like to be tied down by a set of rules and you dislike keeping to a schedule. These people tend to have a messier work environment and tend not to focus on one task at a time. They also don't like to make plans and are much more willing to do things last minute.

IMPACT ON YOUR RELATIONSHIP

Conscientious people are organized, orderly and good at planning things. If you score high on this trait and your partner is low, this can still be a good thing. You can be the one that takes charge of the schedules, the planning, and the budgeting. Your partner is likely to appreciate your help since he is no good in these areas. That being said, if you score *very* high on this trait (like me, I score 85% on this trait) you might have trouble if your partner scores below 50%. This is because you may feel like your partner is lazy, doesn't help around the house and that you are doing "all the work".

Be warned that people who score low on this trait are not necessarily "easy-going". They simply don't like to stick to a schedule. The trait of easy-going or go with the flow is categorized as "agreeableness" which we will discuss below. If your partner doesn't like your plans or the way you keep up the house, they won't necessarily just go along with it. If you are very Type A, you are likely to be most compatible with someone who is low-middle on conscientiousness and high on agreeableness.

EXTROVERSION

Extroversion (and its opposite, introversion) are probably the most talked-about of the five. Most people know where they fall on this spectrum but here is a reminder. People who are extroverts have social stamina and the ability to recharge and receive emotional energy by interacting with others. They are outgoing, talkative and charismatic.

People who score low on this trait are more reserved, quiet and like to keep to themselves. They recharge their emotional energy by being alone and partaking in hobbies that don't require other people such as reading a book or playing video games. Introverts struggle with meeting new people and they would much rather hang out with a small group of close friends if they're going to be social.

IMPACT ON YOUR RELATIONSHIP

Partners who are close to each other on the introvert/extrovert spectrum do best. If you are extroverted, you can still date an introvert but ideally, you're only 60% extroverted and your partner is 40%. If two people are on the opposite ends of this spectrum, it can be very challenging. This is because they'll both have a very different idea of what is "fun". The extrovert will likely want to go out, be with friends and socialize. The introvert would much rather have a quiet night at home. If you and your partner are opposites, you have to understand that it's perfectly okay to do things separately. I have a friend who is very extroverted and happily married to a major introvert. She just knows that she'll often have to go to family events or social gatherings by herself. Since she's okay with that, it works out well.

I'll take this time to mention that if you're ok with your partner not agreeing with your lifestyle or way of doing things, this will make you compatible. It's only when you are showing signs of frustration or trying to force your partner to be someone else that you're going to face a rocky relationship that likely won't stand the test of time.

AGREEABLENESS

Scoring high on this trait means that you are a people pleaser and put others before yourself. You are trusting, kind, empathetic and you do your best to make sure that others are happy. You also tolerate all kinds of people and personalities.

People who score low on this trait are not afraid to put their own needs before others. They have little interest in the feeling or needs of others. People scoring low on this trait can also be manipulative and cold-hearted.

IMPACT ON YOUR RELATIONSHIP

Have you ever seen a relationship where one person is whipped, and the other person makes all the decisions? The whipped person is high in agreeableness and the decision-maker is low on this trait. In a perfect world, both partners would have the same score on this trait. This means both partners wear the pants and each one gets to have their say. If you naturally score very low on this trait, your partner should score high so that you complement each other, but not too high that they get taken advantage of.

If your partner scores high and you score low, that makes you the decision-maker. As the decision-maker, it's very important to understand your role. These types of relationships tend to work great within the first few years of dating or marriage but after you've been together for ten years or more, the "whipped" partner starts to get frustrated because they realize that they never get their way.

As the decision-maker, you need to know that you don't get to have your way all the time just because the other person is nice about it. Agreeable people are nice, selfless and easy going but this can easily be taken advantage of. Try not to take advantage of their niceness!

If you are the agreeable one, understand that it's very difficult for your partner to see it your way if he scores low on this trait. It's not that he's selfish, it's just that he has a harder time compromising than you do. Be sure to stand up for yourself but try to limit it to the important things that really matter, so that you don't get into a huge fight over where to go for dinner.

NEUROTICISM

Scoring high in neuroticism means that you are the opposite of emotionally stable. Neurotic people tend to feel worried, anxious and stressed about situations easily. They are also prone to negative emotions such as sadness, irritability and mood swings. Neuroticism is the "glass half empty" kind of personality trait.

Those who score low on this trait tend to see things with a positive lens. They are able to bounce back quickly after an emotional or traumatic experience. They rarely feel sad or depressed and tend to see good in both other people and the world.

IMPACT ON YOUR RELATIONSHIP

Neuroticism is the one personality trait that limits a person's ability to have a happy relationship. Neurotic people make excellent poets, artists and can be successful in many areas. However, scoring high on this trait means that it will be difficult to find satisfaction with a romantic partner.

A study published in Scientific American mentioned: *"...neuroticism is particularly bad for your marriage. In fact, neuroticism is the one personality trait that best predicts marital dissatisfaction, separation, and divorce. If you want to know if a couple will still be together in 10 years, you might want to start by looking at how often both partners feel irritable or experience mood swings."* - (Tannenbaum, 2014)

Remember earlier how I said that it's difficult to change your traits, but not impossible? This is the one trait that you should always be trying to move closer to emotional stability. Doing it for yourself will mean less anxiety, less stress and greater feelings of life satisfaction. Doing it for your partner will mean less arguing, fewer mood swings, and an overall happier relationship. You can start improving your emotional stability (no matter where you land on the spectrum) by focusing on your own self-care.

It's also important not to gloss over what the study above said about neuroticism and healthy relationships. People who tend to see the glass half empty and who overthink and worry are going to struggle in relationships. If you naturally experience these traits, it's going to be in your best interest to find a partner that is overall positive and light-hearted. A partner like this is going to help you see the bright side of things and help make you feel better. A partner who is just as neurotic as you, or even more neurotic will be more likely to bring your mood down and make you worry more than necessary.

I hope these five personality traits have helped you see the importance of finding a partner that is compatible with you. When I talk to my clients about what they want in a partner, they often say that they want the person to have the same interests as them or they want them to look a certain way. Although those things are important and can be the icing on the cake, the true meat of a relationship is the compatibility of the couple's personalities. If you are a very neat and tidy person and like to keep the house clean, it's going to drive you nuts if you're with a man who leaves a huge mess everywhere and never cleans up. This is going to be a much bigger cause of resentment in your daily life than if he doesn't enjoy going to the same restaurants as you. Looking at a potential relationship like this is very important. You have to understand that relationships are not about the vacations you take or the dinners you go out on once a week, they are about the little details that happen every single day. This leads me to the next important point for picking a man that's worth it, his flaws.

HIS FLAWS ARE SET IN STONE

Take a mental list of his flaws, put them in a big bucket and pour concrete over them. Those flaws aren't going anywhere. In fact, they might get worse over time. One thing to remember when you're dating is that people *can* change but they very rarely do. Think about one of your bad habits, something you have been wanting to change for years.

Have you been able to change it? If you have, was it easy? Most of us have goals. We want to lose weight, get in better shape or wake up earlier and no matter how hard we try, it can take years and the utmost dedication before we see anything happening– and this is for just one or two of the goals we *want* to change. Imagine a man who plays a lot of video games, does he really want to stop doing that just for his girlfriend? Does a man really want to start making the bed every morning just to please his significant other? When you are in a new relationship, just remember that all his flaws are going to be a lot more "forgivable" now that you're just falling in love. You have to be good at trying to see how much you'll be able to tolerate certain things day after day, year after year.

If you think you'll be ok with a flaw and be able to tolerate it, that is a step in the right direction. Let's take the video game example that I mentioned earlier. See, my boyfriend will play video games for the *whole day*. He will wake up in the morning, start playing and then continue to play them until we head to bed. Sure, he'll take breaks once in a while, but he can do this all day no sweat. Now a lot of women I know might get annoyed by this. They might start to nag him and ask him why he needs to do this for the *whole day,* but I don't do that. I *never* do that because it actually doesn't bother me one bit. Now, this is a "flaw" of his that might not sit well with other women, but it's perfectly fine with me.

Take a look at your new man's flaws and ask yourself if you can put up with them forever. People don't really change and if they do, it's a bonus, not a requirement. True love is accepting someone's entire being, including their flaws.

When you start analyzing and thinking if you can tolerate certain things or not, try to think about how important they really are in the long-term. For example, if one of his flaws is that he doesn't like traveling but he is checking off all of the other boxes, you have to think whether that one flaw is worth throwing everything away despite him being nearly perfect in every other way. You can always travel with the girls and know that you have a loving and caring husband to come home to. It's something to consider.

HE DOESN'T NEED TO BE YOUR "EVERYTHING"

There's only so much you can ask for in one person. This is something many women forget. So many of my clients want one person to fill all the roles in their life. They want an exercise buddy, a travel buddy, a cooking partner, financial security, a good father, a masculine guy, an easy-going guy, a good listener, an alpha, a big heart, the list goes on and on. Remember how great your life was being on your own? Doing your own thing? Well if he doesn't want to go traveling, skiing, or be your exercise buddy, there's nothing wrong with doing those things on your own or with a friend. You are a strong independent woman and you don't need your man by your side for every single hobby or interest that you have.

If you spend all your time trying to find a man who shares all your common interests, you might risk forgetting about the important traits that really matter. The ones that determine whether or not you guys are going to be compatible for the long haul.

PRIORITIZE THE IMPORTANT STUFF

You have your checklist of things that you're looking for, and I'm totally on board with that list, but you have to make sure that the list doesn't miss any of the important categories. Things like, he accepts you for who you are, he makes you laugh, he is trustworthy and a good communicator. Those are a lot more important than many of the things I see my clients prioritizing. Some checkboxes that shouldn't be prioritized as much you think include:

- Height
- Hobbies/common interests
- Taste in music or movies
- Dietary preferences (vegan, vegetarian, etc.)

Even things like political opinions are only as important as you make them. Being together forever is a lot of "live and let live." Differences are only as big of a deal as you make them. I know a couple where the man is a meat eater and the woman is vegan and they are perfectly happy. Quick, close your eyes for a second and just imagine how on earth this couple manages to make it work. Picture a happy man and a happy woman. They are making dinner in the kitchen. The woman is cutting up veggies and preparing some rice, while the man is baking some portobello mushrooms and some chicken breast in the oven.

When it comes time to serve the meal, the man grabs the chicken breast for himself and scoops some mushrooms onto a plate for his wife. The two enjoy the meal, chatting and making jokes about their day. It seems rather simple, doesn't it? Yet while talking to my clients, I have heard so many men and women say that they can't be with a vegan or they can't date someone if they eat meat because we "need to be able to share food". This are real comments I have heard from my clients. If you're making something small into a big deal, it's going to be a big deal. If you just decide to accept a difference in someone then you increase your chances of finding a great partner who you're really going to love. I'm not saying you shouldn't have deal-breakers; I'm just saying it's important to pick the right ones.

NOTICE YOUR FEELING PATTERNS

This is the most important way to know if you are dating someone who is worth becoming your long-term partner. All that stuff that I was saying about checkboxes and all that, only comes into play after you have this part figured out. A relationship is only good if it makes you feel good.

How many times have you been in a relationship where you were just going through the motions and acting like a couple but really, deep down you knew something was off? This means that your "feeling patterns" were negative and no matter how many boxes he checked or how "right" the relationship seemed, it couldn't be saved. The ability to pinpoint when you feel a certain emotion is an excellent way to determine the source or cause of those emotions. Your boyfriend should be the cause of healthy and happy feelings 99% of the time.

Keep a mental note of how you feel when you're around your boyfriend. Do you feel negative emotions when in his presence? Feelings like anxiety, stress or rejection? Or do you feel positive emotions? Like comfort, security, acceptance, support. Also, take a mental note of the conversations you have with your new man. These are examples of healthy conversations:

- Humour: Making jokes, telling each other a funny story.
- Playful: Talking while giving each other kisses or tickling
- Practical: Figuring out plans for the weekend or what to eat for dinner.
- Helpful: Asking for help or giving advice on a topic.
- Visionary: Talking about the future and plans for where the relationship is going.

These are examples of unhealthy conversations:

- Bickering: Arguments that stay small and they don't blow up into fights. Usually about petty things.
- Criticism/judgment: Negative comments about your body, your clothes, your taste, possessions, etc.
- Nagging: Sharp, quick comments about what you should be doing or that you're doing something wrong.

- Lecturing: One person calls the shots and tells the other person what to do but the other person doesn't have a say.
- Name-calling or insults: Calling each other derogatory terms or using profanity or harmful language.

Now every couple will dip into the negative side of things once in a while but this should be on the very rare occasion and name-calling or insults should never happen. Interactions should be healthy and happy 90% of the time. Pay attention to how you feel with your partner most of the time and that will be a great indicator of what the rest of your life is going to look like.

HOMEOSTASIS

Homeostasis is a biology term. It means the *state of equilibrium between interdependent elements*. Interdependent elements just mean pieces that work together. Take your body for example. All the organs in your body are working together. When your body is in homeostasis, it means that everything is healthy and working properly. When your body goes out of homeostasis, like when you have a cold, your body is desperately trying to get back to its "normal" or its "homeostasis."

Every relationship will also have its own homeostasis or state of "normal". This is the state in which the two of you are *most of the time.* Take a look at the homeostasis or the normal of your relationship with your new man. Does it make you feel happy? Safe? Excited? Or does it make you feel anxious, like you're walking on eggshells, or like he has one foot out the door?

When I was in an unhealthy relationship, my normal was extremely damaging. My normal was to come home to someone who wouldn't talk to me, wouldn't eat dinner with me and then we would go to bed at separate times. The problem with this homeostasis or "my normal" was that it was *familiar.* It being familiar made it comfortable. Our bodies love things that are familiar. When I was a kid, my mom would make us Cheese Whiz and jam sandwiches as a treat. Yes, Cheese Whiz and jam. I know it's weird and I know it's disgusting – for *you.* The thing is, even to this day that sandwich sounds like a delicious treat to me. It might be gross to you but because it's familiar and reminds me of my childhood, it tastes good to me. Comfort and familiarity feel safe, even when they are damaging. This is why people stay in relationships that are not good for them. It's because change is scary, and familiarity is safe.

This familiarity feeling can work in weird ways. If you have had bad relationships in the past, entering into a new one that still has those bad traits can feel *familiar* and therefore trick your brain into thinking that it's right. When you're out there looking for a new man, you have to remember that you're trying to find that man that is worth your time. The diamond in the rough. If he is showing signs that you *know* are warning signs or red flags. You have to fight the urge that it may feel familiar and see it for what it is, a potentially damaging quality.

Once you find a man where your feeling patterns are healthy and happy and your homeostasis feels good, you know you've found someone who is really worth it, and trust me, it's worth holding out for this man.

INFLUENCE ON YOUR KIDS

When asking yourself if you should continue seeing a man, you should consider your future children. Even if you don't want to have kids, this is a really good mental exercise to see if the man you're with is going to be good for the long-term. See, we have an instinct to protect our offspring. We want to keep them safe at all costs and so we make sacrifices or work extra hard for them. We would also never want to put them in situations that we put ourselves in. We seem to have a shorter fuse when it comes to what we tolerate for our kids than for ourselves and using this instinct on your relationship can be very revealing.

Even if you don't plan on having kids, imagine a future child that is yours. The person you are dating is going to be their dad. They will look up to their dad and imitate him in many ways. They will also have his genes so a lot of his personality traits will be genetically ingrained into them. Ask yourself, if my son turned out exactly like his father, would I be ok with that? If my daughter was in a relationship with a man just like this, would I be ok with that? If the answer to this is no, that's a serious issue.

When I was dating a man who wasn't a good fit for me, I would ask myself this question and would dread the thought of my future son becoming exactly like my boyfriend. This was a huge red flag that my relationship wasn't working out, but I failed to notice it at the time.

There is also the possibility that you might not be around one day, and your new man or boyfriend would be in charge of taking care of the kids all by himself. I know that is a Debbie Downer thought, but when we're dealing with things like life-long partners, the "life" part of it starts to get very real. Can you trust him with raising your children? Does that thought scare the living daylights out of you? If your boyfriend is worth your time, these thoughts shouldn't scare you. It should actually be comforting to know that your kids would be in good hands if you were ever not around to take care of them.

LIFE GOALS

This one is essential. The two of you have to be heading in the same life direction. If he talks about making partner at the law firm downtown and you're planning on moving out to the suburbs, these ideals are bound to clash. The two of you should have the same idea of what a perfect life looks like. Here's what should be considered when you're looking at aligning life goals:

- Location of where to live
- Certain type of house you want (ie. apartment, townhouse, farm)
- Having kids or not/number of kids
- Who will be the one taking care of children and who will be the breadwinner? If both will work, are both partners ok with kids being raised by a nanny or day care.
- Ideals around money and finances

These are the non-negotiables. Everything else, like hobbies, political views and even religion are important but are less important than the ones listed above.

The reason the above list is so much more of a priority is because there is no way to compromise on it. You can't have a relationship where one person lives in the city and the other person lives on a farm. You can't have "half a child" or a child that only one person takes care of. Things like religion or hobbies are more flexible. I know many couples who don't share the same religion, but they are able to compromise and make it work. It is important to know the difference between "non-negotiables" and "negotiables" because it helps you figure out if someone has traits that are deal breakers or something you can work through. That's how you find true compatibility.

FIGHTING FAIR

If you have been in a relationship with a man for many years and you are going through hardship and struggle, it is possible to work on your fighting skills and potentially help re-build the relationship. It's a long road of working on communication and trying to get better at a skill neither of you have been working on for most of your lives. It's do-able, but it's for suckers! Those people got hitched and committed to people who did not have healthy fighting styles and because you're single and didn't just settle down for anyone, you are not going to make that same mistake.

When searching for a man who is really worth your time, you are going to take a deep look at the way he handles conflict. When he knows how to fight fair, things get easier. The entire relationship is more fun and feels less like a chore. You know how people always say that relationships "take work?" Well they don't take nearly as much work when two people have learned how to fight in a healthy way. Here are some methods of "dirty" fighting that if you see happening, you should re-consider whether this man is worth it.

Unhealthy Fighting:

- Name calling and insults
- Yelling
- Stonewalling
- Passive Aggression
- Attacking you instead of the problem
- Not admitting being wrong or wanting to accept "defeat"

It's a lot harder to learn to fight fair when both of you have major issues to work on. Here's what a healthy fight looks like:

- Conversation moves forward to a resolution, you don't get stuck going in circles
- Both partners have their chance to speak and be heard
- No name calling, insults or loud voices
- Both partners are honest and open ie. saying something like: "I don't feel like talking about this anymore, but I promise we can pick this up again in an hour when I've calmed down." This is done instead of ignoring or door slamming.

Now nobody is perfect so we may all slip into some bad habits every once in a while, but if your man has a healthy way of dealing with conflict, you'll find it's a lot easier to talk to him when either of you are upset. I learned this lesson only by seeing it play out in front of me.

When my current boyfriend and I got into our first fight, I was surprised at how painless it was.

Although I was upset and cried a little bit, after the whole thing was over, I felt a flood of healthy emotions. I felt supported, listened to, and even *more* attached to him than I did before the fight. Yes, it's true. If a couple is good at fighting fair, they will actually feel closer and more attached to each other after the fight is over. This is so much better than feeling like permanent damage is being done to your relationship every time he leaves the toilet seat up.

THE MONEY ARRANGEMENT

Everyone knows money is one of the most common reasons people get divorced. Money is part of our everyday lives whether we like it or not. If you go for brunch, who's picking up the tab? If you need some more toilet paper, who's got that this time? Who did it last time? If you want to have kids, who is staying home to raise them and sacrificing their financial independence? Who is taking on the burden of financially supporting the household? These are big questions that absolutely need to be asked when you're seeing someone and trying to find out if they are going to be worth your time in the long run.

Many women don't want to be the breadwinner in a relationship, but modern women also love their jobs and don't want to quit just to stay at home with the kids. This is something that you as a woman need to find out what your preference is and then find a man who agrees with the decision that you have made. An article from Business Insider reminds us that these are difficult conversations but very important:

"Successful couples not only discuss the future with open minds, but they reveal their full financial pasts to their partners — even when it's painful. That means revealing every ugly detail about their salaries, credit card debt, student loans, credit score, and anything else that might impact their financial future." (Martin, 2016)

Every single day we are faced with who's going to pay for what and if the arrangement isn't figured out properly, it can be a one-way ticket to resentment.

PAYING ATTENTION TO HIS STORIES

You can learn a lot about a person by what he chooses to talk about. I know that when I am in a conversation with someone there is a huge chance the conversation will end up at movies, real estate, mental health etc. These are a few go-to topics that I enjoy talking about and they are deeply part of my personality. This goes for just about any human. The topics he chooses to talk about are probably some of his most passionate interests. If he's talking about politics, he's probably a news junkie. If he mentions the food and the quality of the food, he could be a health nut or a foodie. Paying attention to the topics that come up when you're around him is going to be a good indicator of what he's interested in but also the middle ground of things that you guys have in common. If you like the topics of his stories and they make you feel happy or interested, this is a good sign.

I am going to give a quick example here from my own life because it was a lesson I learned late in my dating life. I was on a date with a guy who was very intelligent. I enjoyed talking to him because we moved on from small talk quickly and were talking about deep and meaningful things before the appetizers were served. The problem was, I didn't really like where our conversations tended to go. The middle ground of things we had in common just wasn't a place where I was happy to spend my time, it was too heavy.

I am very interested in the intricacies of mental health and so when he started bringing up those topics, I gladly played along. The problem was that the conversation became very heavy, very quickly. We both had analytical personalities and were dissecting and breaking down everything from why humans face depression to the meaning of life. Although I was deeply invested in this conversation and we ended up talking for hours, I walked away from that date feeling drained and almost a little embarrassed. Like I had revealed too much too quickly. Although I am intelligent and enjoy a good logical debate, doing that for three hours was exhausting.

Contrast that to the first date I had with my current long-term boyfriend. That first date also involved some personal topics but the conversations always ended up somewhere fun. Somewhere where we were both laughing or surprising each other or teaching each other something new. I walked away from that date feeling energetic, happy and like I was the funniest, most entertaining woman in the restaurant. This energetic vibe that we were giving each other was a lot more light-hearted, fun and paved the way for a relationship of jokes, laughter and genuinely fun times. This is something you want to be looking out for when trying to figure out if the man you're with is going to be a good partner. You should be asking yourself, how does he make me feel? If the answer to that is a list of good emotions that you want to feel for the rest of your life, you've got a keeper.

THE HONEYMOON PHASE

This chapter has been a lot! It is a lot of things to consider when meeting someone new but one thing I want to remind you is – don't overthink. Although some of this stuff does take some thinking and analyzing, the biggest thing you can do is listen to your gut feeling and have fun. Enjoy this lust, butterfly feeling, otherwise known as the honeymoon phase.

YOU DON'T NEED A MAN!

As you start to come out of the haze of lust and chemistry, then you can start thinking about whether this is going to be a good partnership for the long-term, but this decision should be an easy one to make. If you find yourself questioning a relationship, then something might not be right about it.

When I was in relationships that were unhealthy or ended up going nowhere, I found myself overthinking and trying to "convince" myself that I was doing the right thing. There were a lot of questions and inner turmoil going on in my head. When I found the man that I wanted to be with forever, it felt easy, natural and normal. There was no questioning or second guessing because I just knew it was right. After months of dating and just having fun, I had to put him to the test and see if we logically fit together. I had to ask him where he saw himself living, the kind of life he wanted in the future and the kind of financial situation we would be in. Once those boxes were checked, I knew I had It all. I had something that felt right and made logical sense. This is a conclusion you have to come to after the honeymoon phase is over, so it could take about a year.

THE ORDER OF THINGS

There are two pieces to the puzzle when trying to find a man that is worth your time. You want it to *feel* right and you want it to make sense logically. The key to successful dating and finding a man that is worth your time is to focus on the "feels right" part first and have the logical part slowly reveal itself. This might feel backwards, but it's a much better way to get your priorities in the right place.

When I started dating my current boyfriend, I did not imagine myself leaving the city that I currently live in. I knew that he had thought about leaving our city for a smaller town but he was willing to sacrifice his goals for me, because he loved me. Together we developed a strong relationship and now, three years later, I am prepared to move with him outside of our city. This is because we have the "feels right" part of our relationship totally locked down and it made me reconsider some of the logical stuff.

Now don't get me wrong, you can't expect that someone is going to change their mind about something (like having kids) just because they love you, but the "feels right" part of the relationship is a non-negotiable.

That's the part that you have to make sure is good before you consider compromising.

WHEN TO COMPROMISE

You might be feeling overwhelmed by the giant list of requirements I just gave you for a good man, but I have good news. There are thousands, even hundreds of thousands of men with those qualities out there. The list I gave you isn't that long when we consider the fact that there are 3.5 billion men in the world and you only need to find one.

That being said, we know that the more things you have on your list, the narrower the search pool gets. I have briefly mentioned the places where you can compromise in this chapter, but I wanted to sum it all up in black and white.

Non-Negotiables/Never compromise:

- He must make you feel happy 90% of the time
- Healthy fighting style
- You accept his flaws and entire personality
- He accepts your flaws and entire personality

- Agreement on financial situation
- Similar life goals

Everything else can be worked through and compromised and you can even change your mind on things so that you agree on the non-negotiables. For example, if you want to keep your job but he wants to be the breadwinner so you can stay home then you are not lining up on "agreement on financial situation," making you incompatible. But, if he changes his mind and says that he's fine with the kids going to day care, you just negotiated your way back into compatibility.

Knowing that there is this flexibility between humans is empowering because it makes it less daunting to find a good man and you put a little more control back into your life. Remember, if you have a deal breaker that is set in stone, no one is asking you to change that, but if you decide you want to change something, you can.

IN CONCLUSION

I know this chapter was a lot to take in. Instead of getting caught up on the list of qualities, just put them away. You have now read what you should be looking for in a good man and you don't need to dwell on it. After what you learned in the "mindset chapter" you know that this man is out there and ready for you to find him. Now you know the qualities you are looking for and after reading the "dating game" rules you can act in a way that will lock him down. You're a triple threat! You've got this.

CHAPTER EIGHT

Needs and Wants

WELL, I HAVE HAD A BLAST WRITING THIS BOOK and taking you along this journey. This book has been a long time coming, taking years of research and wisdom gained from clients who told me their stories one on one.

In this book, you have learned about modern relationships, how to deal with your emotions while dating, how to play the dating game and how to find a man that is truly worth your time and has long-term potential.

Taking this logical approach to dating may seem boring and like it's taking the fun out of it, but I can assure you that there's nothing more fun than being head over heels in love with someone who is going to make an amazing addition to your life.

Before we say goodbye, I want to say some final words that are directly for you, the person holding this book. In your life, you have reached goals and accomplishments that are truly amazing. You have overcome hardships and struggles. You've been through bad relationships, both romantic and non-romantic and every time you went through those, you came out stronger. Having baggage, overthinking, fearing intimacy or rejection make you *human*, they do not make you weak. Those things are trying to protect you, but you know that you can handle anything that comes your way. You've done it before, and you can do it again.

When you're looking for a man, you don't want just anyone. You've done perfectly fine without a man and will continue to do perfectly fine if you don't find one that meets your standards. You never want to settle for less than a strong man. One who accepts you for who you are and one who is emotionally stable. He makes *you,* the strong independent woman who takes care of everyone and everything, finally feel like you can be taken care of. Like someone out there has *your* back for a change. Even though you know you don't *need* him, you kind of (just maybe) *want* him.

I wish you the best of luck in your search and if you need more resources or support, visit me at Millennialships.com.

ABOUT THE AUTHOR

Lana Otoya is a professional dating coach and dating advice blogger. Her work has been featured in articles on websites such as "Best Life" and podcasts like "Something You Should Know". Lana is a published author and has written books on small talk, self-confidence, and more.

Lana started her work in the professional dating scene as a matchmaker. Here she saw that dating is very emotionally draining, frustrating and that most men are flaky and do not take the lead. Using both a scientifically based approach to dating and the experiences of her one on one clients, she developed strategies to help women find men who are serious and worth their time. She considers herself a strong and independent woman and wants to help women like herself find a man that truly enhances their life rather than settling down just to be married.

If you'd like to learn more about Lana's work or sign up for her coaching sessions, visit her website at Millennialships.com

Your Free Gift

Don't get stuck with a loser again!

Download my FREE *Dating Red Flags Checklist* so you know how to look for a high quality man.

Visit: millennialships.com/red-flags

Works Cited

Adams, R. (2014 May 5). *If You Feel Bad About Being Single It is Not Becauae You're Single.* Retrieved from Huffington Post https://www.huffingtonpost.ca/2014/05/01/being-single-happiness-women_n_5007469.html

Bloom, L. a. (2017, 13 July). *Want More And Better Sex? Get Married And Stay Married.* . Retrieved from Huffpost: https://www.huffpost.com/entry/want-more-and-better-sex-get-married-and-stay-married_b_5967b618e4b022bb9372aff2

Brown, B. (2010, June). *Power of Vulnerabily.* Retrieved from Ted: https://www.ted.com/talks/brene_brown_on_vulnerability#t-577712

Cleveland Clinic. (2019, February 2). *Women and Stress.* Retrieved from Cleveland Clinic: https://my.clevelandclinic.org/health/articles/5545-women-and-stress

Deborah Carr, V. A. (2014, October 1). *National Centre For Biology Information.* Retrieved from Happy Marriage, Happy Life? Marital Quality and

Subjective Well-Being in Later Life : https://www.ncbi.nlm.nih.gov/pmc/articles/PMC4158846/

Gottman, J. (2010, June 11). Can You Really Predict Divorce? (KCTS, Interviewer)

Hermanson, M. (2018, July 3). *How Millennials Are Redefining Marriage.* Retrieved from Gottman: https://www.gottman.com/blog/millennials-redefining-marriage/

Jacobs, T. (2017, October 10). *New Evidence That Women Are Less Selfish Than Men.* Retrieved from Pacific Standard: https://psmag.com/news/new-evidence-women-are-less-selfish-than-men

Jesse, C (n.d.) This Is How Many Couples Who Met On Dating Apps Are Getting Married: https://www.theknot.com/content/how-many-dating-app-users-get-married

Livingston, A. (n.d.). *Financial Benefits of Marriage vs. Being Single – What's Better?* Retrieved from Money Crasher: https://www.moneycrashers.com/financial-benefits-marriage-single/

Martin, E. (2016, November 11). *The most important financial decision you can make to have a successful marriage* . Retrieved from Business Insider: https://www.businessinsider.com/most-important-financial-decision-for-successful-marriage-2016-11

Mental Health Foundation. (2013). *Mental Health Statistics: Relationships and Community*. Retrieved from Mental Health Foundation: https://www.mentalhealth.org.uk/statistics/mental-health-statistics-relationships-and-community

Rabin, R. C. (n.d.). *Put a Ring on It? Millennial Couples Are in No Hurry* . Retrieved from New York Times: https://www.nytimes.com/2018/05/29/well/mind/millennials-love-marriage-sex-relationships-dating.html

Riper, T. V. (2006, July 25). *The Cost Of Being Married Versus Being Single*. Retrieved from Forbes: https://www.forbes.com/2006/07/25/singles-marriage-money-cx_tvr_06singles_0725costs.html#672abf637269

Roberts, A. (2018, February 14). *Sex and finances are better for married people* . Retrieved from CNN: https://www.cnn.com/2018/02/14/health/valentines-day-single-married-comparison-trnd/index.html

Schwartz, D. J. (1959). *The Magic Of Thinking Big* . New York: Simon and Schuster.

Science Daily. (2014, July 25). *Why do men prefer nice women? Responsiveness and desire* . Retrieved from Science Daily: https://www.sciencedaily.com/releases/2014/07/140725110757.htm

Stanley, S. (2015, February 11). *How To Lower Your Risk Of Divorce: Advice To Singles* . Retrieved from Institute For Family Studies : https://ifstudies.org/blog/how-to-lower-your-risk-of-divorce-advice-to-singles

Tannenbaum, M. (2014, February 14). *Sex and the Married Neurotic* . Retrieved from Scientific American: https://blogs.scientificamerican.com/psysociety/sex-and-the-married-neurotic/

Tigar, L. (2019). *How Men And Women Fall In Love.* Retrieved from Ask Men: https://ca.askmen.com/dating/dating_advice/how-men-and-women-fall-in-love.html

Wang, S. (2008). *Your Brain Lies To You* . Retrieved from New York Times: https://www.nytimes.com/2008/06/29/opinion/29iht-edwang.1.14069662.html

YOU DON'T NEED A MAN!

Made in the USA
Monee, IL
26 February 2023

28737965R00121